Air-launched Doodlebugs

Air-launched Doodlebugs

The Forgotten Campaign

Peter J.C. Smith

First published in
Great Britain in 2006
By Pen and Sword Aviation
An imprint of
Pen and Sword Books Ltd
47 Church Street,
Barnsley,
South Yorkshire
S70 2AS

Copyright © Peter J.C. Smith 2006

ISBN 1-84415-401-7

A CIP record for this book is available from the British Library

Front cover painting © Keith Woodcock 2006

Typeset in 10/12pt Palatino
by Mac Style Ltd, Scarborough, N. Yorkshire

Printed and bound in Great Britain
by CPI UK

Pen and Sword Books Limited incorporates the imprints of Pen and
Sword Aviation, Pen and Sword Maritime, Pen and Sword Military,
Wharncliffe Local History, Pen and Sword Select, Pen and Sword
Military Classics and Leo Cooper.

For a complete list of Pen & Sword titles please contact
PEN & SWORD BOOKS LIMITED
47 Church Street, Barnsley, South Yorkshire, S70 2AS, England
E-mail: enquiries@pen-and-sword.co.uk
Website: www.pen-and-sword.co.uk

CONTENTS

Introduction

n a spirit of euphoria the *London Evening News* of Thursday 7 September 1944 announced:

> *London's 80 Days: The First Full Story.*
> *8,000 Fly Bombs Came Over:*
> *Only 9 per cent Reached London in Last Days:*
> *Defences had 2,000 Balloons, 2,800 Guns:*
> *The Battle is Over says Duncan Sandys.*
> *The first full story of the Battle with the flying bombs in which 92 per cent of the fatal casualties were in London is revealed today.*

Duncan Sandys with General Sir Frederick Pile, the Chief of anti-Aircraft Command, on his right and Air Marshal Roderic Hill in the foreground, makes the ill-timed announcement of 7 September, saying, 'Except for a last few shots the Battle of London was over'. Events were to prove him very wrong. (US National Archives)

Mr Duncan Sandys MP, Chairman of the Flying Bomb Counter Measures Committee revealed that during 80 days' bombardment 8,000 flying bombs were launched, of which 2,300 reached the London area.

The story tells of a Gun Belt which stretched from Maidstone to East Grinstead so as to screen London and how it was decided later to move the entire Anti-Aircraft Belt down to the coast so that the guns should have an uninterrupted field of view. In the first week 33 per cent were brought down and the same proportion reached London, whereas in the last week 70 per cent of the bombs were brought down by the defences, the others being inaccurate or erratic.

Then came a note of hesitation: 'Except possibly for a few last parting shots, what has come to be known as the Battle for London is over, said Mr Sandys, who disclosed that flying bombs were also launched from aircraft, the Heinkel 111 being specially adapted.'

Seated alongside Duncan Sandys at the press conference upon which the newspaper report was based were the two officers credited with the acclaimed defeat of the eighty-day flying bomb offensive: Air Marshal Roderic Hill (afterwards Sir Roderic), Chief of the Air Defence of Great Britain Organization, and his army deputy Lieutenant General Sir Frederick Pile.

As it transpired the claim was premature. The air-launched flying bombs which Duncan Sandys dismissed so lightly as 'a few last shots' were to increase in number and become a potentially serious menace. These and the V2 rockets, the first of which was to land in the London area the following day, were to make life in the capital dangerous for another seven months.

Mr Sandys' 'few last shots' remark was directed specifically at the flying bombs, since the rockets were not then known. *Vergeltungswaffe* 1 (V1 for short), missile, flying bomb (fly for short), Fiesler 103, FZG 76, doodlebug (bug for short), pilotless aircraft (PAC for short), robot, chuff, diver or simply bomb, were all terms used to denote a weapon in the form of a small jet-propelled pilotless monoplane bomb in which the Nazi leadership placed faith as a counter to the increasingly heavy Allied air raids on Germany.

After it finally came into use in June 1944, the weapon did cause a great deal of damage, both in Great Britain and in Belgium, before its operations finally ceased at the end of March 1945. Whilst the great majority of the V1s were launched from ramps, a specially equipped bomber unit III/*Kampfgeschwader* 3, later expanded and renamed *Kampfgeschwader* 53 was formed to launch the missile from under the wing root of the Heinkel 111 aircraft and this development enabled the Germans to continue flying bomb attacks on Britain after the Allied occupation of their launching sites in northern France.

This facilitated a guerrilla campaign using the forerunner of the cruise missile. The approach and target could be switched at any time. The way in which this campaign developed, was countered and finally defeated is set out in the following pages.

Acknowledgements
I wish particularly to thank Frank Leyland of Crumpsall, Manchester, and Bob Collis of Oulton Broad, Suffolk, who have greatly assisted me with material for inclusion in this book. My thanks also to the many other people who have helped me, but who are too numerous to be listed individually.

Developments at Peenemunde

The British victory in the Battle of Britain in the late summer of 1940 put an end to large-scale daylight raids on Britain. Through the winter and into the spring of 1941 heavy night raids were made but the German invasions, first of the Balkans then of Russia, drew the bulk of the *Luftwaffe* away to the Eastern Front in what Adolf Hitler expected would be a temporary measure. Germany's bomber force, however, was destined never to return in real strength to the Western Front.

Before the outbreak of war, in September 1939, Hitler appointed himself both head of state and supreme commander of the German armed forces, so that his orders whether political or military would prevail. It was with increasing frustration that he beheld, from 1942, a progressive increase in the weight and effectiveness of British and American air attacks, whilst he was unable to respond adequately.

German minds were therefore directed towards an alternative long-range weapons technology. The occupation of the French shore of the English Channel made bombardment of southern England look feasible. Indeed, two very long-range railway-mounted guns, 21 cm K12s based on the design of the First World War 'Paris Gun', were moved up to the Channel coast in 1940. These guns each weighed 302 tonnes and fired a shell weighing 107 kg (236 lb). They had a maximum range of 115 km (71 miles), and one shell almost reached Chatham, Kent. The barrel wear was so great, however, that the monsters were seldom used. There was therefore a need for the German armaments industry to replace the absent

A 21 cm K12 German railway gun used from the summer of 1940 to August 1944 to bombard the extreme south-east of England. Excessive barrel wear precluded more than occasional use of these monster weapons. (*Bundesarchiv*, Germany)

bombers and the ponderous guns with weapons able to strike cheaply and effectively against targets in Britain.

In the event two such weapons were developed and used operationally. They were later given the generic name

Germany's failure during its rearmament to develop a heavy bomber gave rise to an urgent need as the war evolved. The Heinkel 177 was chosen to meet this need but its revolutionary Daimler Benz 610 engines proved too complex. V weapons then became the only means to sustain a viable air offensive against Great Britain. (Imperial War Museum)

vergeltungswaffen ('revenge weapons') by the German propaganda media. *Vergeltungswaffe* 1 (V1), a flying bomb, was a jet-propelled pilotless winged missile carrying an explosive warhead of 850 kg (1,874 lb) and *vergeltungswaffe* 2 (V2) a liquid-fuelled rocket with a 1 tonne payload.

It was not only lack of available aircraft that frustrated the *Luftwaffe* bomber effort in the west after mid-1941. The earlier need to build a numerically superior force for pressing political reasons dictated that they concentrate on manufacturing small and medium bombers, primarily those with a dive-bombing capacity. By 1939 this expansion had been largely achieved and the changing political scene later suggested a need for a heavy long-range bomber. The dive-bomber concept was by then so deeply rooted that the specification issued for it encompassed a dive capability.

The heavy bomber chosen for development was a Heinkel design, the He 177. Over three years of valuable time was absorbed in its development, and the only German purpose-built heavy bomber of the Second World War never went into large-scale production, owing largely to technical problems arising from a faulty original specification. In some measure this was offset by the

Erhard Milch (right) was the driving force behind the development of the V1 flying bomb, which he saw as the Luftwaffe *response to the army's development of the V2 rocket.* (Milch collection)

emphasis on the unconventional V weapons as the means of delivering the much sought after offensive capability.

A research and experimental weapons establishment was set up following the joint purchase by the army and the *Luftwaffe* in 1937 of the north-western peninsula of the 'island' of Usedom on the Baltic coast. A nearby fishing village called Peenemunde gave the experimental station its name. At the tip of the peninsula an airfield was constructed under the name of Peenemunde West or Karlshagen.

Whilst the army, in its share of the establishment, experimented with long-range rockets which culminated in the successful A4, later called the V2, the *Luftwaffe*, on its side, later developed, amongst other weapons, the V1 flying bomb.

In the late spring of 1942 General Erhard Milch, the Secretary of State for Air and Inspector General of the *Luftwaffe*, was invited to view what turned out to be a highly successful launching of the A4 rocket. So envious was he of the army's triumph under Werner von Braun and Colonel Dornberger, who claimed that their rocket would have range enough to bombard London from continental bases, that he called an urgent meeting of the Scientific Committee of the Air Ministry, of which he was the chairman.

At this meeting, which was held on 10 June 1942, Dr Fritz Gosslau of Argus Motorengesellschaft, Berlin, described the success of experimental work previously carried out by himself and Dipl. Ing. Paul Schmidt on the practicability of a cheap ramjet engine. He suggested that this could become the motive power of an effective flying bomb. This accorded exactly with the *Luftwaffe*'s requirement for the propulsion of an expendable aircraft.

Milch showed such enthusiasm for the idea that a formal requirement was issued for an expendable, automatically piloted aircraft with range enough to reach London from the French coast. The idea of a pilotless aircraft was by no means new; it having been tried as early as the First World War. The novelty came in the revolutionary technology which was about to be brought together for the first time in order to meet the *Luftwaffe*'s requirement.

Gerhart Fiesler, a First World War pilot who had become an aircraft manufacturer of high repute, was required to draw up a general specification and outline scheme to meet the overall requirement. This was accepted by the *Luftwaffe* high command, and a team of engineers and contractors was appointed under the control of Dipl. Ing. Lusser. They commenced work on the detailed design of the fuselage and control system. The Fiesler Aircraft

Manufacturing Company was made responsible for the project as main contractor. In accordance with German aircraft industry practice the machine was given the title Fi (for Fiesler) 103. To disguise its purpose for security reasons it was also entitled *fern zeil gerat* ('long-range target apparatus' – FZG) 76.

The development of one of the key components, the cheap, easily mass-produced automatic pilot, was placed in the hands of Askania Werke AG of Berlin. This company was amongst the foremost German precision instrument manufacturers and had in 1933 been licensed by Sperry Gyro Inc. of Brooklyn, USA, to manufacture and sell their automatic pilot system. Sperry had furnished the technical data, tools and production drawings to get Askania started.

Argus Motorengesellschaft meanwhile undertook the development of the ramjet propulsion unit on which so much depended.

In June 1943 unpowered dummies of the Fi 103 were dropped from a Focke Wulf 200 at Peenemunde and proved aerodynamically satisfactory. These were shortly followed by two drops from a Heinkel 111 H-6 fitted with a carrier pylon to test the control surfaces of the missile, and it was concluded that the fundamental design was right.

Between 22 and 28 August 1943, tests using the Heinkel carrier were made with fuelled missiles under power and one of these proved almost too successful; it overshot its intended range and fell on the Danish island of Bornholme and some of its secrets were gathered by Danish resistance sympathizers and passed on to the Allies. Several also strayed onto Swedish territory during trials and some construction details gleaned from these reached Britain. During tests in September altitude was maintained over a distance of 120 km, but the directional mechanism still gave trouble.

On 6 April 1944 trials began at Karlshagen to determine the most satisfactory carrier aircraft, for General Milch favoured the operational use of the air-launch method 'for the purpose of deception'. Strangely the stated failure rate during these early air launching trials was as low as 16 per cent.

The whole assembly was designed for simplicity, mass production and interchangeability of parts. The need to avoid the use of scarce resources in construction was remarkably well handled by the designers.

While the Argus ramjet motor was well suited to its purpose it was highly inefficient in energy use. For every mile of flight it consumed a gallon of petrol, as much as that used by an RAF

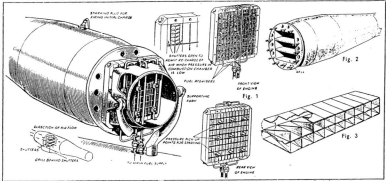

OCTOBER 19, 1944   245   THE AEROPLANE SPOTTER

AEROPLANES IN DETAIL—LX

VERGELTUNGSWAFFE EINS (FZG. 76)

PROPULSION UNIT.—(Fig. 1.) The drawing shows the forward end of the hollow propulsion unit. Fuel feeds, shutters, fuel atomizers, shock absorbing support and the sparking plug, which ignites the initial charge, are clearly illustrated. Immediately behind the shutters is a grille (Fig. 2), the only venturi in the entire motor. The light alloy intake valves and the steel strips, which open according to the pressure inside the propulsion unit are shown in Fig. 3. They are very small, the diameter of the unit at its maximum being only 1 ft. 10½ ins.

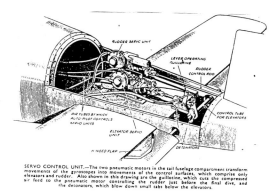

SERVO CONTROL UNIT.—The two pneumatic motors in the tail fuselage compartment transform movements of the gyroscopes into movements of the control surfaces, which comprise only elevators and rudder. Also shown in this drawing are the guillotine, which cuts the compressed air feed to the pneumatic motor controlling the rudder just before the final dive, and the detonators, which blow down small tabs below the elevators.

Two of the key mechanisms of the V1, the pulse jet and the tail surface's servo control unit, as revealed in the Aeroplane Spotter journal of 19 October 1944. (The Flight Collection)

Lancaster bomber whose four piston engines developed nearly 6,000 hp. To the petrol consumed there must be added an expenditure of compressed air, some 50 litres. The very simplicity of the ram or pulse jet therefore came at a price in high fuel cost.

    The operating cycle of the ramjet began with the release of compressed air into the petrol tank. This forced a fine spray of petrol into the forward and widest part of the propulsion tube through a set of three banks of atomizers with three spray nozzles in each. Here it was mixed with air and detonated at the start of the launch by a spark plug activated through a cable from a power supply in the Heinkel carrier plane.

The air for mixing was provided by the forward thrust of the missile, initially under the wing of the Heinkel but later by its own forward thrust. This air entered the forward end of the propulsion tube via multiple rows of light spring steel valves, each shaped like a clothes peg and set between the banks of atomizers. The explosion of the petrol–air mix in the propulsion tube had the effect of forcing the valves to close momentarily, causing the combustion gas to vent through the tapering rear of the tube and thus thrusting the unit forward. The cycle then resumed, but after launching the residual flame inside the propulsion tube was sufficient to ignite further

Taken from a technical film sequence, this was taken to record the performance of the missile on air-launch trials over the Baltic Sea near Peenemunde. (Deutches Museum, Germany)

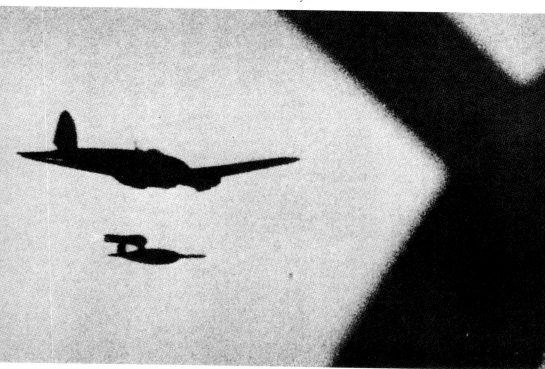

injections of fuel–air mix. The cycle was designed to repeat forty-two times per second.

The spring steel inlet valves, despite a protective baffle, were eroded by the heat and flame of the combustion so that the efficiency of the ramjet tended to reduce as the flight proceeded. This was one reason for the variation noted in missile speed. In normal circumstances the small progressive loss in motor efficiency as the flight proceeded was offset by the reduction in weight of the missile as the petrol and compressed air were consumed.

The average airspeed of a V1 was around 360 mph, but it could vary between 250 and 400 mph in extreme cases. A minimum launching speed of 150 mph was needed to enable the pulse duct tube to work properly and to carry the missile away without stalling. A motor which had been running for longer before release would stand a better chance of a successful launch.

One common misconception regarding the V1 is that the motor always cut out at the commencement of its terminal dive. The control mechanism was indeed designed to achieve this. It was activated by an air log called *zahlwerk*, which measured the distance flown and at a preset range both severed the compressed air pipes operating the control surfaces and released spoiler flaps under the tail surfaces, causing the bomb to spiral down. Once the compressed air escaped, the petrol tank became depressurized and no more fuel reached the ramjet. A distinct whine was sometimes heard from the falling missile as the compressed air escaped.

If, as sometimes happened, however, this mechanism failed to operate properly or the missile was damaged, it could come down under power. It was also found that some robots were not fitted with the explosive devices needed to operate the guillotine and the spoilers of the *zahlwerk*. They depended on the far less accurate ranging method of simply putting a set amount of petrol into the tank, leaving the bomb either to glide or fall when it ran out. Damage caused by defensive fire was also a common reason for erratic V1 behaviour.

Air-launch trials carried out over the Baltic off Peenemunde not only established the feasibility of the method, they also showed that the best German aeroplane then available for the purpose was the tried and reliable, if obsolete, Heinkel 111, numbers of which were readily to hand. On the face of it, the V1 appeared to be an unwieldy load for the aeroplane to carry and launch from the air. The method adopted was the only one feasible: the flying bomb was suspended from a shallow pylon mounted under the wide wing root, as close as possible to the centre line of the aeroplane.

During early trials the missile was hung under the port wing but during training and on operational flights the starboard wing root was used. Initially it was expected that the handling characteristics of the asymmetrically loaded plane, particularly during take-off, would be made difficult, even hazardous. Surprisingly, pilots reported that the stability was not unduly affected when carrying a V1 and that the take-off did not present any undue problems, being accomplished in 800–900 metres. The drag caused by the missile, once airborne, was corrected by trimming the rudder about 1 degree. The speed of the Heinkel at a height of between 100 and 200 metres was reduced by about 20 kph (12½ mph) compared with the unladen speed.

The fuel-carrying capacity of those Heinkels converted to the air-launching role was fixed at 3,460 litres (761 gallons) which gave them an endurance of five and a half hours, adequate to cover the maximum expected flying time of four hours.

The air-launch flying bomb Heinkels are frequently referred to as H-22 versions. Strictly speaking, however, only those converted on the production line from H-21 variants are H-22. Most of the Heinkel 111s adapted into the role were H-16 or H-20 variants and these were referred to by the old mark classifications in German reports.

Information on enemy activity at Peenemunde filtered through to Britain, much of it from Polish forced labourers held there, through a well-directed 'underground' organization. This led to RAF reconnaissance flights over the site and to a series of heavy British and American bombing raids, commencing with a major attack on August 1943.

In early 1944 the third *Gruppe* of the German bomber unit *Kampfgeschwader* 3 (III/KG 3) was selected for air launch training and moved to Karlshagen airfield for this purpose. A cadre of *Luftwaffe* personnel who had been involved in the experimental work was formed into a training unit known as *Erprobungskommando Karlshagen*. They instructed the III/KG 3 crews who attended a ten-day conversion course, involving three flights each of one hour. The pilot alone was instructed on the first of these and no V1 was carried. The bomb aimer meanwhile received about half an hour's instruction on the ground in the operation of the release gear.

On the second flight a flying bomb without a live warhead was carried and the whole crew flew, accompanied by an instructor.

During this flight the starting, aiming and release procedures for the missile were practised. On the third and last training flight the crew practised a launch on their own without an instructor present. The trainee crews competed with each other in aiming a missile which was tracked down the Baltic Sea firing range by German radar.

Completing their course on 10 June, the first III/KG 3 crews trained were posted to airfields in northern France with the intention that they should take part in the opening of the V1 campaign against England. When this got off to a hesitant start two or three days later, however, it became obvious that the air-launch crews were not yet ready to contribute.

Meanwhile a reduced experimental section equipped with several adapted Heinkel 111 H-6 aircraft continued work at Karlshagen and are recorded as having tested flying bombs with various modifications. On another occasion they used a modified Junkers 188 bomber experimentally, but this made a forced landing and testing was discontinued. The section gradually faded from the scene thereafter.

CHAPTER TWO

III/KG 3 in France

With high expectations Field Marshal Keitel, Hitler's chief of the high command, issued a directive for the opening of the flying bomb campaign against England on 16 May 1944. This stated:

The *Führer* has ordered:

1. The long-range bombardment of England will begin in the middle of June. The exact date will be set by the Commander-in-Chief [C-in-C] West, who will control the bombardment with the help of LXV Army Corps and Third Air Fleet.
2. The following weapons will be employed:
    (a) FZG 76
    (b) FZG 76 launched from Heinkel 111
    (c) long-range artillery
    (d) Bomber forces from Third Air Fleet.

The LXV Army Corps was set up on 15 December 1943 to direct the V weapon campaign and was under the command of Lieutenant General Erich Heinmann. It was composed of both army and *Luftwaffe* personnel, with its headquarters at Saint Germain on the outskirts of Paris. III/KG 3 in France passed under its operational command but administrative command was exercised by the Third Air Fleet, which covered the north-west of France.

The operative *Luftwaffe* Staff Order stated, 'III/KG 3 remains assigned to *Luftflotte* 3, which will ensure smooth co-operation between LXV Corps and III/KG 3. HQ LXV Corps will forward air requirements to *Luftflotte* 3. C-in-C West has overall command.'

III/KG 3 was composed of three *staffeln* (squadrons), 7, 8 and 9, under a *gruppe* headquarters. It was allocated to three airfields to the north of Paris: Beauvais/Tille, Parmain/L'Isle Adam and Roye/Amy. Whether these housed individual *staffeln* or were used by the whole *gruppe* in rotation is not known. An agent's report received by British intelligence later reported seeing an air-launch aircraft at Roye/Amy.

Keitel's directive for the opening of the V1 campaign was over-confident. In the early morning of 13 June a single pilotless aircraft (PAC) fell at Bow in London, one of only ten launched. It was not until Thursday the 15th that the campaign began in earnest. On the opening day some thirty-three long-range shells were fired across the Channel, some of which fell in the Maidstone area but there was no air launching or conventional bombing. Disaster, however, struck III/KG 3 on 16 June when a chance air raid on Beauvais/Tille by US Air Force (USAAF) B-24 bombers destroyed eight Heinkel carrier aeroplanes on the ground.

Uncertainty exists over the early operations of the air-launch aircraft but it was noted from British radar tracking of approaching doodlebugs during late June and early July that a few were already at operational height when first located. This suggested that they were not climbing to height from the ramps but were probably air launched on the same course for London. This supplement to the ramp launches may be regarded as operational training for III/KG 3 crews. Their first clearly identifiable operation took place on the night of 9/10 July when the German tactics changed, to the confusion of the defenders. Launching on this occasion took place from the east towards London. Nine missiles came in up the Thames estuary. Air Marshal Hill, Chief of the Air Defence of Great Britain (ADGB) organization and Lieutenant General Sir Frederick Pile, commanding the anti-aircraft (AA) guns, had by that time devised a plan to redeploy the AA guns to the coast in a 'belt' opposite the launching ramps. The move took place over the period 14–17 July and was a major success, giving the guns an unrestricted opportunity to shoot down the divers over the sea.

An Air Scientific Intelligence Report – No. 151 – of this time makes reference to 'intercepted supply returns from certain airfields in northern France giving the compass settings for flying bombs. These lay between 264 and 356 degrees, indicating that the coast line from Fécamp (22 miles NW of Le Havre) to Walcheren had been used.'

One week after the opening of the doodlebug campaign an enemy agent planted in London had been discovered and turned by the British counter-espionage service. On instruction he signalled that there was considerable flying bomb damage in Southampton. This was a main supply port for the Allied bridgehead in Normandy. The German LXV Corps HQ staff were much puzzled, as there had been no attempt to bombard the port. They therefore presumed that a few missiles intended for London had been misdirected or gone astray. Nevertheless they were attracted to the prospect of hitting the Allied supply route through Southampton.

Covertly, therefore, twenty-two flying bombs from the ramps were deliberately aimed at the port. Field Marshal Von Rundstedt, the C-in-C West, then received a warning from Hitler's HQ ordering a cessation of this diversion. Soon afterwards he was replaced by the more pragmatic Von Kluge who approved an attack on the port but limited it to air-launched flying bombs.

III/KG 3 carried out the attack, spreading it over four nights in the second week of July. An examination of the plots of those doodlebugs which fell on land shows that the ranging was fairly good but that the direction was less accurate. Seventy-three per cent fell into a narrow ellipse measuring 8 × 33 miles, with its centre positioned about 8 miles north-east of Southampton. There was some doubt in British circles as to whether Southampton or Portsmouth was the target of these attacks but the fact that 50 per cent of the impact plots are contained within a circle with its centre about 3 miles south of the mouth of the River Itchen removes any doubt as to the intended target.

The night of 10/11 July
The raid took place after midnight and twenty-two doodlebugs came within range of the defences. AA fire shot down three over the sea and four over land. Night fighters destroyed two over the sea and one over land.

Overland missiles fell at:

Alresford
Beaulieu, in the New Forest, 7 miles south-south-west of
    Southampton
Brockenhurst, in the New Forest, 10 miles south-west of
    Southampton
Two at Bishops Waltham, 9 miles north-east of Southampton
Two at Curbridge, 7 miles east of Southampton
Dummer, 4 miles south-west of Basingstoke
East Boldre, 10 miles south-west of Southampton

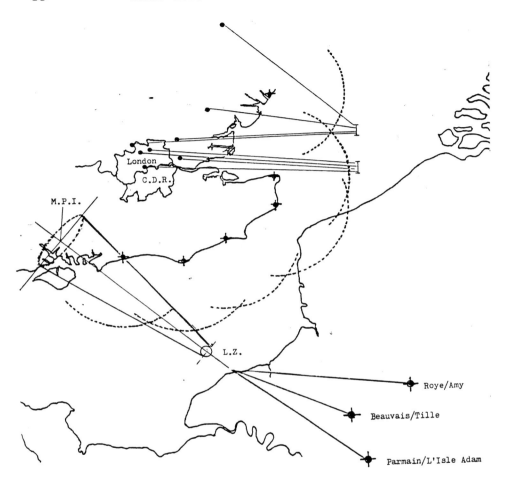

London
C.D.R.

M.P.I.

L.Z.

Roye/Amy

Beauvais/Tille

Parmain/L'Isle Adam

0   50   100 Miles.

A map showing the operations by III/KG 3 against London on 9/10 July and (opposite) against Southampton between 10 and 15 July. (Frank Leyland)

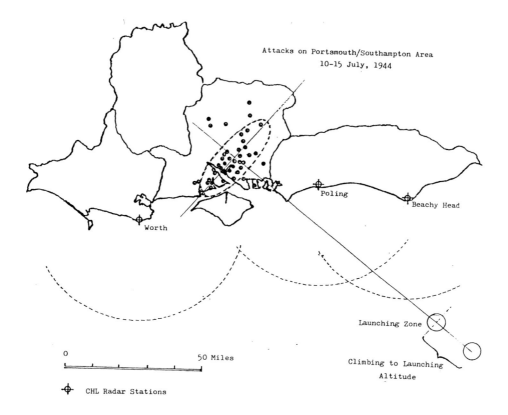

Attacks on Portsmouth/Southampton Area
10-15 July, 1944

Poling

Beachy Head

Worth

Launching Zone

Climbing to Launching Altitude

0   50 Miles

CHL Radar Stations

Exton, 12 miles north-east of Southampton

Fareham, on the north-west side of Portsmouth Harbour, 6 miles from Portsmouth

Hookpit

Netley, on the northern bank of Southampton Water, 3 miles from Southampton

Pooks Green on the southern bank of the River Test, 3 miles south of Southampton

Shedfield, 8 miles east of Southampton

Upham, 10 miles north-east of Southampton.

Since only sixteen divers were plotted as impacting on land, it appears that one of those destroyed must have exploded in the air and was therefore not recorded by civil defence authorities.

The night of 11/12 July
Just before dawn fourteen flies came within range of the shore defences, which must have been taken off guard for only two were shot down, both into the sea by AA fire.

Impacts were recorded at:

Beaulieu
Bentworth, 7 miles south-south-east of Basingstoke
Bitterne, in Southampton. Nine people were injured and ten houses damaged
Botley, 5 miles east of Southampton
Brockenhurst
Burlesdon, 5 miles east of Southampton
Chandler's Ford, 4 miles east of Southampton
Dibden, 2 miles south and on the other side of Southampton Water
Fair Oak, 6 miles north-east of Southampton
Fawley, on Southampton Water
Longwood, 12 miles north-east of Southampton
In the River Test, south of Southampton.

The night of 13/14 July
This smaller raid came in some time after midnight. Only three divers were reported on land. They fell at:

Durley, 7 miles east-north-east of Southampton
Itchen Stoke, 5 miles east-north-east of Winchester
Sutton Scotney, 7 miles north of Winchester.

The night of 14/15 July
The final raid of the four came in about two and a half hours after sunset, placing it between 00.30 and 01.30 hours. Thirteen divers impacted ashore, one of which caused the worst flying bomb incident of this brief series, in Portsmouth.

These fell at:

Beaulieu
Catharington, 10 miles north-north-east of Portsmouth
Cheriton, 7 miles east of Winchester
Eastleigh, 5 miles east-north-east of Southampton
Froxfield, 16 miles north-north-east of Portsmouth
Goodworth Clatford, 18 miles north of Southampton. This fell

between the Royal Oak pub and the village school,
demolishing both. Six people were killed in the village

Kilmeston, 14 miles north-east of Southampton

Chandler's Ford

Portsmouth. Fifteen people were killed and ninety-eight injured
when extensive damage was done at Newcomen Road,
Stamshaw

Southampton, Sholing. Here six people were injured, one of them
seriously, when severe damage was done to sixteen houses

Warnford, 15 miles north-east of Southampton

West End, just east of Southampton on the east bank of the River
Itchen

Worting, Basingstoke.

As a result of the Southampton attack, Lord Cherwell, Winston
Churchill's scientific adviser, wrote to Herbert Morrison, the Home
Secretary and Minister of Home Security, suggesting that he might
take the pressure off the people of London by encouraging a
diversion of missiles to Southampton. 'I would press you to
consider the possibility of commiserating with a south coast town
on the damage done, indicating that the attack (on Southampton)
had been a success.' Morrison replied that 'politically it would be
dangerous in the extreme' and moreover 'it would be known to be
untrue and doubts would be cast on the accuracy of government
statements generally'. A few further flies fell in the Hampshire area
after 15 July but these were strays from the ramp launches against
London.

Operating out of their French airfields to a launching zone some
miles off the coast between Fecamp and Dieppe, clear of detection
by British coastal radar stations, involved III/KG 3 aircraft in a
round trip of between 140 and 220 miles. Whilst this was hazardous
in view of the Allied air supremacy, it did not result in any losses
of aeroplanes.

The best available estimate of the number of air-launched divers
directed at Southampton is ninety. Of these about one-third were
abortive launches. The approach up the Solent into Southampton
Water, along the eastern shore of the Isle of Wight, caused some
disturbance, as one lady in Ryde reported.

*The first time they came over we did not know what on earth was
happening. The sirens went when I was in the kitchen with Granny
making a cup of tea before going to bed. Immediately after the siren
ceased wailing there was a roar like an express train outside and a plane*

came over the house at a tremendous speed, very low. It was followed by a second one right on its tail. There was a loud bang in the distance, then silence. These were the flying bombs that up till now we had escaped.

The total number of launchings carried out by III/KG 3 from French airfields is difficult to gauge but was probably about 180, including those aimed at Southampton. The British authorities were aware from intercepted radio traffic that air-launch training had taken place at Karlshagen and that III/KG 3 was the unit involved. They also became aware that it had moved to French airfields. The first newspaper to pick up the fact that flying bombs were directed against London from the east following the 9/10 July trial raid was the *Daily Sketch*, whose issue of 13 July commented under a speculative minor headline, 'Flying Bombs from Belgium'.

A stray air-launched V1 intended for Southampton on 15 July struck the village of Goodworth Clatford at 1.05am. The school and the Royal Oak public house were both destroyed along with The Thatch, a private property. Mr and Mrs William Jones, their 17 month-old baby and Mrs Sylvia Church were killed. In nearby Manor Farm Cottages Miss Ellen Tatford and Mrs Florence Watton died. (Unknown)

The operations from French airfields were short lived and came to an abrupt end after 15 July when Allied troops began to break out of Normandy. The time had anyway come to move to airfields better placed to follow up the 9/10 July operation, outflanking the AA gun belt and its associated defences.

The night of 9/10 July

British radar located and tracked at least some of the first flying bombs to approach the coast from the east. Four good tracks were plotted and when extrapolated appeared to have crossed the enemy-occupied coast near Blankenberge close to the Dutch/Belgian border. The tracks were roughly parallel, indicating a good directional setting. On account of the distance flown and the fact that no launching sites were known to exist in the area, air launching was suspected, but it was not confirmed for some time.

At 02.17 hours one of these flies impacted at Colledge Farm, Ovington, 8 miles south-west of East Dereham in Norfolk, causing no casualties but doing minor damage, mainly to windows.

Three other flies are thought to have reached London but cannot be clearly distinguished from ramp-launched ones coming from France on the same night. Four more which are distinguishable fell at:

Gosfield, 2 miles west of Halstead, Essex
Ongar, Essex
Upminster, on the eastern edge of London
Radlett in Hertfordshire.

CHAPTER THREE

Withdrawal to Holland

Dutch airfields at Venlo and Gilze-Rijen were chosen as the main bases from which III/KG 3 were to conduct air-launched flying bomb operations against London. They were well placed for the purpose, being on an east–west alignment with the Thames Estuary. Venlo lay 280 and Gilze-Rijen 220 miles from London.

The air-launch tactics used were determined by the capabilities of the British coastal radar, of which there were two complementary systems, Chain Home (CH) and Chain Home Low (CHL). The former used taller transmitting and receiving towers and a longer wavelength transmission, and could detect plots at longer ranges, often over 100 miles. For technical reasons, however it would not respond to low-flying aircraft. CHL augmented CH in this respect and was able reliably to detect low flyers over the sea within its range using a shorter wavelength transmission. The range of CHL was normally 40–50 miles.

In order to conceal the Heinkels as much as possible, a low-level approach was adopted. Flights were made at 300 metres when over land approaching the coast, dropping to 100 metres over the sea. For security reasons barometric altimeters were used, with only an occasional check using the aircraft's radio altimeter. A flying speed of 170 mph was maintained.

On approaching the launching zone the aircraft climbed to a height of 500 or 600 metres; during the climb the airspeed fell to about 110 mph. On levelling out the airspeed was built up to not less than 170 mph, the stalling speed of the V1 being 150 mph. The

Heinkel was aligned to the V1 course setting chosen, which was also that preset in the directional compass of the missile. The Argus ramjet of the fly was started up and allowed to run for ten seconds before release, which was signified in the aeroplane by a cessation of the vibration from the ramjet and a lift as the weight of the bomb fell away.

During the start-up of the jet and in the ten seconds before the release of the missile the Heinkel was lit up like a beacon, and its crew felt very vulnerable to night-fighter attack. Hans Hoehler, who flew as an aircrew member on several later missions, described it as like 'sitting in a lighted bus for all to see'. Having released their load the crew were very ready to corkscrew back down to 100 metres to make their escape. The official advice was to follow the missile for a short period before dropping down in order to deceive night-fighter crews.

Navigation was not really a problem during these short flights over the sea, roughly parallel to the Dutch and Belgian coast. Flashing two-letter coded marker beacons were placed at the coastal crossing points on Walcheren or near Blankenberge, visible for the short periods necessary for operations. Both fixed searchlight beams and prearranged flak bursts have been mentioned as additional aids to navigation.

Such was the haste with which III/KG 3 became operational after the move to Holland that advance parties of ground crew probably made preparations before 16 July. British intelligence sources became progressively more aware of the air-launch threat and reality. A report drawn up for the Chief of Air Staff (CAS) on 31 July stated: 'Flying bombs have been launched from the sea area Ostend-Dutch Islands'. Under the heading 'Activity' it declared: 'These first appeared from the Dutch islands on 9/10 July. Launchings from the area have been fairly regular and on a gradually increasing scale since 18/19 July, culminating in 22 [sic] last night. In all 131 appear to have been fired from this area – all between 23.30 and 04.00 hours.'

The next day the Assistant Director of Intelligence (ADI) – Science concluded that the radar tracks 'starting from Belgium were in fact those of flying bombs launched from Heinkel 111 aircraft of III/KG 3'. He also noted a report from an agent confirming this method of launching from observation. The relevant part of the agent's report, translated from the French, spoke of 'launching of V1 by aircraft over Knocke Bains [near Blankenberge] coming from the east and flying towards the west'.

On 7 August a further report made reference to 'launching of airborne flies from the Low Countries' and stated: 'In the absence of other evidence intelligence assume that the fix of launching points is done by dead reckoning but Lorenz beams, visual or radio beacons would be the easiest plan.' The report listed advantages that the enemy may gain from air launching: flexibility, rapid rate of fire from the same bearing, avoidance of forward bomb dumps and lessened shock to the missile on launching.

Air Intelligence (AI3B) issued a document on 31 July which listed radio intercepts of particular interest. These included various messages from carrier aircraft engaged in launchings 'over the Dutch islands and the Ostend coast'. The list connected known flying bombs to these aircraft flights. One message mentioned the destruction of a Heinkel 111-SVI FZG76 at Karlshagen and another the unit concerned, III/KG 3 at Venlo. The document went on to speculate that a single *gruppe* of thirty Heinkel 111s would give the enemy only limited scope but that it was quite possible that operations on a much wider scale against other targets might be envisaged. The scale of training activities at Karlshagen, of which British intelligence became aware through radio intercepts, certainly supported this belief in a significant expansion. The key to much of this intelligence gathering lay in the ability to decipher coded Ultra messages.

A succession of raids by III/KG 3 from Holland, aimed at London, commenced on the night of Tuesday, 18/19 July, and nine were carried out by the end of the month. These generally proved to be effective attacks, launched before the air defence of London was properly adjusted to meet them. The launching zones off Walcheren Island, Blankenberge and Ostend were easily located by the crews involved.

There was confused speculation in Allied circles as to the mechanisms and precise methods used by the Germans. Interpretation of aerial photographs of Venlo airfield revealed III/KG 3 Heinkels, but without any distinguishing features. Eager for leads the photographic interpreters latched onto one reconnaissance cover taken on 27 July, which they claimed showed a Heinkel with 'an object approximately twenty feet long above its fuselage extending from the nose to a point above the trailing edge of the wing'. This they suggested was 'light coloured and might possibly be a protective cover over some fitting on the fuselage'. This appeared to match the fact that an Allied agent reported seeing 'a twin-engined aircraft believed to be discharged when near its

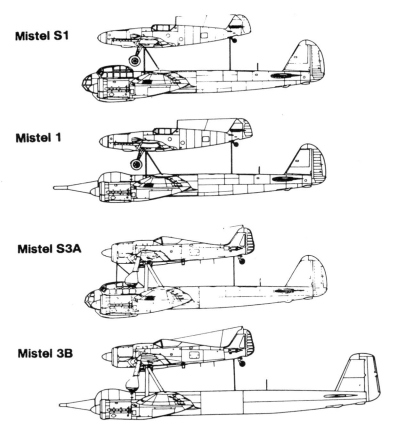

Mistel S1

Mistel 1

Mistel S3A

Mistel 3B

A totally different air-launched flying bomb, the Mistel, was under development during the second half of 1944 and this confused British intelligence sources into a belief that the V1 was launched from a position above the carrier aircraft. In the case of the Mistel, the unmanned explosive-packed lower component was aimed and launched at the target by the pilot of the upper aircraft which itself was intended to return to base. The unwieldy character of the Mistel severely limited its use against Britain. One however, coded ST+CK exploded at 23.35 hrs at Slade Bottom Farm, Binley near Andover, Hants on 10 August 1944. Two more were employed on the night of 1 September. At 23.30 hrs one is reported to have detonated at Warsop, Notts. Another at 23.45 hrs made a crater 12 feet deep and 40 feet across at Hothfield, near Ashford in Kent.

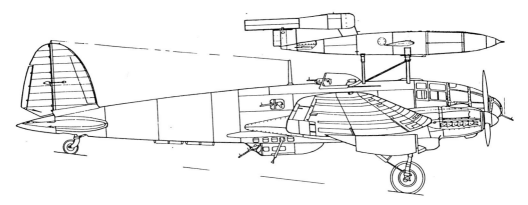

The imagined pick-a-back flying bomb as it was envisaged when air launching was first suspected by the British authorities. (Frank Leyland)

target and directed by wireless' – probably a Mistel combination, a totally different flying bomb concept using two aeroplanes. This confusion led to the early surmise that the air-launched V1 was probably supported on some sort of cradle above the carrier plane. This was picked up by the British press, who were familiar with the pre-war mail plane combination of flying boat and float plane called Mercury-Maia. Early press illustrations therefore showed this conjectural arrangement.

The night of 18/19 July
After its diversion to Southampton III/KG 3 again turned its attention to London in a very accurately directed raid starting shortly after sunset. British radar returns indicated that some eighteen launches took place and by extrapolation of the tracks found that these came from the Walcheren Island/Blankenberge coast.

Incidents included a V1 exploding in a lane beside Gipping Wood, Gipping, Suffolk, 14 miles east of Bury St Edmunds at 22.27 hours. There were no casualties but some damage was done to Wood Farm. Air-launched flying bombs reached the London area, falling at Barnet, Cheshunt, Enfield, East Ham, Fulham, Hackney, Poplar, Southall and Southgate. Others reported at Kimble Wick in Buckinghamshire and Hythe End in Berkshire could have been air launched but this is uncertain from the records.

An Ultra radio intercept report stated that Heinkel 111s of KG 3, 'the third *gruppe* of which is known to be associated with V1', had been destroyed at Karlshagen.

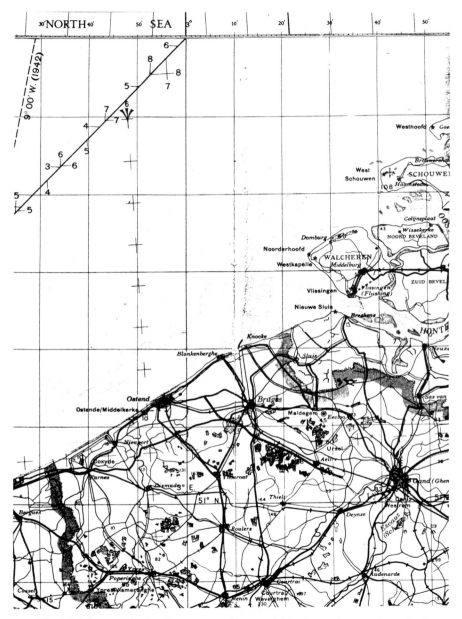

The Walcheren-Blankenberge coastal area which the earlier air-launched flying bomb carriers crossed on their sorties, from an RAF flying map of 1944. (Crown)

The night of 19/20 July

Radar tracking indicated eleven 'missiles', running roughly parallel to each other, crossing the enemy-held coast between Blankenberge and Nieuwe Sluis, whilst four others crossed Walcheren Island.

Altogether, radar tracks suggested a total of twenty-four launchings, starting half an hour after sunset and again well directed. These appeared to originate from two separate launching zones.

London districts struck were:

Chingford
Ealing
Enfield (two missiles)
Edmonton (also two missiles)
Feltham
Hammersmith
Poplar
Tottenham.

In Essex three doodlebugs came to earth, at:

Epping, 17 miles north-east of central London
Ingatestone, 24 miles north-east of London at 00.08. This did
    extensive damage to The Hyde and twenty-five other houses.
Stow Maries, 9 miles south-east of Chelmsford.

The night of 21/22 July

Good radar tracks of thirteen missiles were plotted approaching the Thames Estuary, but only ten reached the coast. Nineteen launches were estimated, divided into two groups, one of which passed through the north of Walcheren, the other to the south of it.

Two of the missiles hit London, one at Enfield the other at Cheshunt. The others fell in Essex at:

Billericay
Epping
Gallywood, 3 miles south of Chelmsford
Hockley, 5 miles north-west of Southend
Steeple, on the south side of the Blackwater Estuary
Kelvedon Hatch, 19 miles north-east of central London
Little Stambridge, 5 miles north-north-east of Southend
Rainham, 2 miles south-east of Dagenham.

The night of 23/24 July
The raid took place about two hours before sunrise, which put it at about 04.00 hours. Bombs reaching the London area fell at:
    Chigwell
    Enfield
    Ilford
    Waltham Holy Cross
    Willesden.

In Essex there were shortfalls at:

    Shenfield, near Brentwood
    Maldon
    Creeksea, a mile south-east of Purfleet
    Nettleswell, a built-up area south-west of Harlow.

Two penetrated into Hertfordshire, coming down at Sacombe, 9 miles north-west of Harlow and at Watton, 6 miles south-east of Stevenage.

The night of 24/25 July
An attack came in at about 23.00 hours, an hour after sunset. There were impacts in London at:

    Cheshunt
    Edmonton
    Ealing
    Hendon
    Hammersmith
    Wood Green.

One missile fell at Lower Nazeing in Essex, 3 miles south-west of Harlow. Three struck Hertfordshire at:

    Hertford Heath in Hertford
    Meesden, 7 miles north-west of Bishops Stortford
    Standon, 6 miles west of Bishops Stortford.

The Meesden and Standon flies were seen to pass over the coast close together near to Felixstowe.

The night of 25/26 July

This attack started at about 04.15 hours and radar returns indicated that eleven missiles were launched. Three reached London at:

Chigwell
Hornsey
Walthamstow.

Another three fell in Essex at:

Hastingwood, on the outskirts of Harlow
Pilgrim's Hatch, 3 miles north-east of Brentwood
Rettenden, 9 miles north-west of Southend.

Three more reached Hertfordshire at:

Welwyn
Gilston, just north-west of Harlow
Cuffley.

The night of 26/27 July

Radar returns suggested that 8 flies were air launched, but there is insufficient data available to separate them from ramp-launched ones.

The night of 30/31 July

Ultra intercepts provided British intelligence with solid confirmation of air launchings. From instructions transmitted to flak units on the Dutch coast, it was possible to build up a picture of the operations of III/KG 3 for the night.

The following flights were notified to German defences:

Nine He 111s outward flight 23.25 hours, inward about 23.50 hours off Blankenberge.
Eight He 111s outward 02.55 hours, inward about 03.15 hours off Blankenberge, height 200 metres.
Three He 111s outward 02.55 hours Walcheren, inward about 03.30 hours at Schouwen, height 150 metres.

British radar returns showed flying bombs approaching from the Ostend-Dutch islands area:

23.35–00.15 hours, ten flies from the Ostend area
03.24–03.50 hours, twelve from the Dutch islands.

Comparing the times given, the operation of the He 111s roughly paralleled the flying bomb effort which radar recorded.

The appearance was of two separate raids. All times recorded were adjusted to the British double summer time then in use.

London was severely hit again at:

Friern Barnet
Ealing
Fulham
Harrow
Hornsey
Hackney
Wembley
The City.

Two fell in Essex at:

Kelvedon, 12 miles north-east of Chelmsford
Stanford Rivers, 12 miles west-south-west of Chelmsford.

Before finally concluding that the flying bombs coming from the east were air launched, the British authorities stated that altogether 131 'had been fired' from this direction. They prepared statistics to show the accuracy of these in terms of range and direction. The range deviation averaged 5.3 miles and the line deviation 4.8 miles, indicating a fairly high degree of accuracy.

They also listed the measures taken to locate the source of the missiles: radar; shipborne radar provided by the Admiralty; photoreconnaissance; a search for shipborne ramps; and agents' reports.

A very much reduced level of air-launch activity during August may have been due to a build up of resources for the longer nights and more favourable operating conditions of early autumn.

The night of 2/3 August
A single attack was made at about 02.45 in a strength indicated by radar returns as fifteen launches. Missiles reaching London fell at:

Edmonton
Brentford
Hayes
Wembley
Staines.

One was shot down by AA fire at Ostend near Burnham-on-Crouch, Essex.

The night of 21/22 August
An attack started about two hours after darkness fell. Divers struck London at:

Brentwood
West Ham
Willesden.

In Hertfordshire there were incidents at:

Colney Street, 3 miles south of St Albans
Wheathampstead, 6 miles south-east of Luton.

One missile fell at Pirbright in Surrey, and another at Hartlip in Kent. The latter crossed the Isle of Sheppey and the north Kent marshes at Upchurch. By the time it reached Hartlip it was flying very low so that it struck the top of some trees and exploded near the detached farm cottages known as the Roman Villas. A woman was killed here but her son and daughter survived with injuries.

The 28 August issue of the London *Evening Standard* reported 'More V-Weapon Launching Sites Captured'. In mid-August Colonel Watchel's ramp-launching crews of Flak Regiment 155 (W) began to evacuate the launching sites on his left flank as the advance of the Allied troops came close enough to threaten their capture. This left only those in the Pas de Calais still in action. As the Allied advance speeded up, the orderly retreat of 155 (W) became a rout. By the last days of August only one battery remained in action. It fired its last missiles in the early hours of 1 September and then joined the retreat.

The night of 29/30 August
British radar returns reported air launchings, of which seven bombs crossed the coast. Two of these hit London, out of a total of nine

doodlebugs to fall on the capital that night. Another two were reported as falling in Essex, at Stapleford Tawney, 13 miles north-east of central London and at Nazeing. One fell at Brill, 10 miles west of Aylesbury in Buckinghamshire. The other two have been confused with those launched from ramps and are untraced.

The night of 30/31 August
This night is shrouded in some mystery. The authoritative work *Defence of the United Kingdom*, written by Basil Collier with semi-official backing states that twenty-one flying bombs were air launched towards Gloucester. That city is however about 150 miles from the nearest point to the East coast, the Thames Estuary. Thus conventional doodlebugs with a 150 mile range could not have been started from the usual launching zones, some 40 miles off the coast. V1s with a range of about 200 miles would be necessary to reach Gloucester.

Such extended range missiles were developed and used against the UK during March 1945, and some evidence suggests that they may have been used as early as August 1944 in small numbers. The fact remains, however, that no flying bomb fell anywhere near to Gloucester.

Between 04.33 and 04.45 V1s were recorded as flying from east to west over Felixstowe and impacts were reported at:

Near Moor Bridge Farm, Harleston, 3 miles west-north-west of Stowmarket, Suffolk, at 04.45 hours. Seven people were injured here when four houses were damaged.
Raydon, 8 miles south-west of Ipswich, where two houses were demolished.
Great Wenham, 7 miles south-west of Ipswich, where no casualties were caused but some damage was done to a farm.
Chapel St Mary, south-west of Ipswich. A garage and five houses were damaged.

The night of 4/5 September
The final raid of the first phase of air launching came as a single attack about one and a half hours before dawn and lasted for some thirty-five minutes. The launching zone was roughly opposite Felixstowe. Nine flies crossed the coast, with the following effects:

Marshes beside the upper reaches of the King's Fleet Dyke on Candlet Farm near Felixstowe at 05.08 were hit with no casualties or damage

Eyeworth, near Biggleswade, in Bedfordshire was damaged at 05.30

Langham, 7 miles north-north-west of Colchester was damaged at 05.35

Flying Officer K.V. Panter of 501 Squadron flying Hawker Tempest No. 551 coded SD-S shot down a diver which he saw approaching at 1,000 feet and 400 mph at 05.40. He got into position as it crossed the coast and later opened fire from 250 yards astern. It crashed at Aldham, 7 miles west of Colchester

Little Bardfield, 8 miles north-west of Braintree, Essex at 05.50. Flying Officer R.C. Deleuze, flying Tempest coded SD-Z of 501 Squadron shot down a fly at Dedham, 7 miles north-east of Colchester at 5.50.

Three fell in Hertfordshire at:

Kings Walden
Stagenhoe
Ware.

The Allied advance rolled on. British troops entered Brussels on 3 September; it was time for III/KG 3 to withdraw.

CHAPTER FOUR

Operation *Rumpelkammer*, Phase 2

The code name chosen by the Germans at the start of their V1 campaign, Operation *Rumpelkammer* (literally translated as 'Junkroom'), was left rather bare after the launching ramps were abandoned. Not all was ruined, however, for III/KG 3 had conducted a so far successful attack without loss of aircraft to enemy action, except those destroyed in the fortuitous air raid on Beauvais-Tille on 16 June. It was ready and able to carry on Operation *Rumpelkammer* on an increasing scale.

In early September, radio intercepts made by the British Y Service showed an increasing level of air-launch training activity at Karlshagen, which was correctly interpreted as an intention to expand the air-launched V1 campaign. Politically, however, the Government's view at the end of the eighty-days summer attack was sanguine. On 5 September a congratulatory letter went out from the Secretary of State for Air. Full of confidence, he wrote to Air Marshal Roderic Hill:

I am commanded by the Air Council to convey to you their warm congratulations on the manner in which the defences against the flying bombs have operated since the launching of the enemy's campaign against London and southern England.

The council have watched with admiration the steadily mounting rate of destruction inflicted on flying bombs. They are aware that this result could only have been achieved by the most careful planning and by imaginative development of the defences to meet each phase of the attack as it developed. The measures, coupled with the devotion to duty of all concerned with the operation of the fighters, of the manning of anti-aircraft guns, the balloons and the air-raid reporting organization, largely crippled the enemy's effort and achieved what can only be described as a notable victory.

I am to request that the contents of this letter may be brought to the notice of all concerned in your command.

Organizationally a German *kampfgeschwader*, roughly the equivalent of an RAF group, was made up of three *gruppen*, each equivalent to an RAF wing. A *gruppe* was divided into three *staffeln* (squadrons), each consisting, when up to strength, of from nine to twelve aircraft, complete with aircrew, technical ground staff and general-duties men. At any one time only a proportion of the nominal strength in aircraft would be serviceable, the others being under repair or scheduled maintenance. For III *gruppe* the *staffeln* were numbered 7, 8 and 9. Both *geschwader* and *gruppe* headquarters staff included members who took part in operations, flying in headquarters flights, as well as being involved in command and administrative duties. In the *Luftwaffe* a separate airfield administrative organization called *Luftgau* provided a number of important services to resident units.

Between 5 and 15 September III/KG 3 established itself at designated airfields in the north-west of Germany: *Gruppe* HQ, along with 8 *Staffel* at Schleswig, 7 *Staffel* at Leck and 9 *Staffel* at Eggebek. All three airfields were situated towards the Danish frontier. Phase 2 of Operation *Rumpelkammer*, the phase without simultaneous ramp launches, was about to begin. In this phase the V1 was to be used in support of the V2 rocket campaign, which coincidentally opened against London on 8 September.

Operating from the more distant German bases and the prospect of worsening winter weather to come, together created a navigational problem. To help solve it, improved navigational equipment became available. Each of the III/KG 3 Heinkel 111s was sent from its Dutch airfield to Nieder-Syferdorf by Grottau in Germany for the equipment to be fitted before being flown on to its designated operational German base. Only when an air-launch-equipped Heinkel was finally captured in April 1945 at Kohnblissen did the Allies have an opportunity to examine it. Code named *Zyclops*, the system involved three powerful radio transmitters set up on the Dutch coast at Den Helder, Zandvoort and Alkmaar. The one at Den Helder acted both as a coastal crossing marker on which

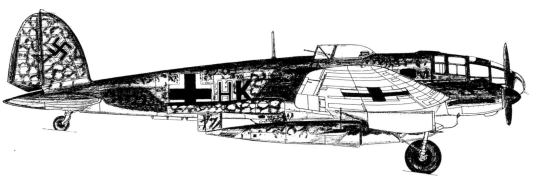

The zahlwerk *rod of the Heinkel with a small windmill propeller at its tip can be seen projecting from the leading edge of the starboard wing, well clear of any aerodynamic disturbance.* (Frank Leyland)

Against the ramp-launched doodlebugs during the summer the barrage balloon proved an effective screen, accounting for well over 200 missiles. Feared interference of the balloon cable with the gun-laying radar sets was given as the reason for the balloons not being deployed north of the Thames during the air-launch phase. (Imperial War Museum)

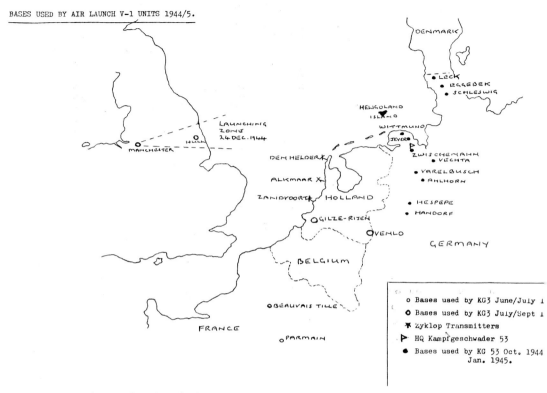

BASES USED BY AIR LAUNCH V-1 UNITS 1944/5.

o Bases used by KG3 June/July 1
◖ Bases used by KG3 July/Sept 1
✸ Zyklop Transmitters
▶ HQ Kampfgeschwader 53
● Bases used by KG 53 Oct. 1944
                 Jan. 1945.

A map showing the bases used by the air-launched flying-bomb units and the positions of the Zyclop radio transmitters, particularly that at Den Helder used by the air-launching Heinkels as a start up indicator for the Zahlwerk *air log.* (Authors map)

to trace dead reckoning navigation to the designated launching zone and as a start point for a preset air log in the aircraft. British air intelligence speculation that a Knickbein type of directional radio beam was involved proved incorrect. Such a beam was not necessary for such a short over-sea flight and the very low operational altitude anyway precluded its use.

The radio operator was able to mark the instant the aircraft overflew the transmitter and trigger the count-down of the preset air log, called *zahlwerk*. On approaching the launching zone which was indicated by the figure 1,000 appearing on the dial of the *zahlwerk* control box panel, the pilot began his climb to launch

Mr Sandys's claim on 7 September that 'except for a last few shots the battle of London is over' quickly proved itself to be a false dawn.
(London Evening Standard)

height. He turned onto the course setting for the target and the bomb aimer commenced the launch procedure by starting up the pulse-jet motor of the missile. When the figure 0 appeared on the *zahlwerk*, the bomb was released.

The tachometer mechanism of the *zahlwerk* was driven by the rotation of a small two-bladed windmill propeller situated at the forward end of a tube jutting out from the leading edge of the right wing of the aeroplane, well outboard of the engine. The tube was long enough for the *zahlwerk* propeller to be turned in the undisturbed slipstream. Thus the number of revolutions counted by the tachometer measured the distance flown since the start-up of the *zahlwerk*, fixing the release point.

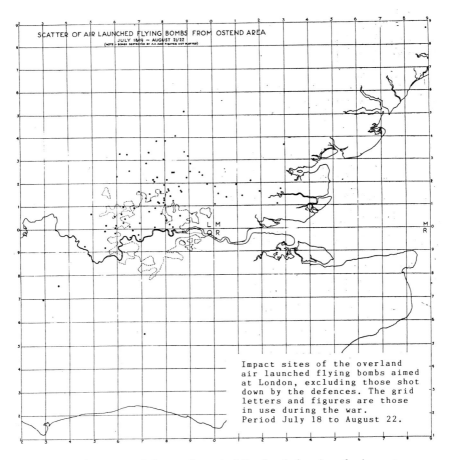

Impact sites of the overland air launched flying bombs aimed at London, excluding those shot down by the defences. The grid letters and figures are those in use during the war. Period July 18 to August 22.

Comparative maps of the south-east of England showing the impact locations of air-launched doodlebugs, excluding those shot down by the defences, for the periods 18 July–22 August and 15 September–15 November.

For all its technology the system did not produce the expected results. Maps drawn up by British intelligence plotting the impact sites of the air-launched flying bombs despatched before 15 September show that almost all impacted north of the Thames and within a compact radius of about 25 miles. Those launched during the second phase, after that date and using the new technology, had a wider spread, some falling as much as 50 miles north of London and some 40 miles south.

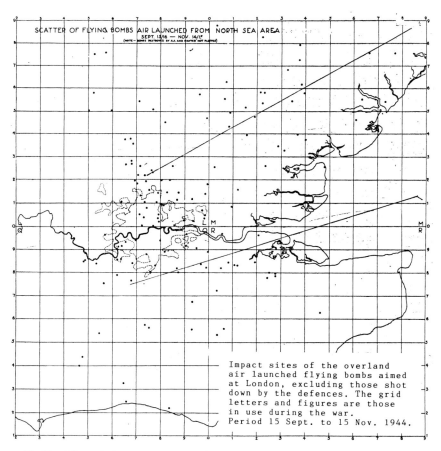

SCATTER OF FLYING BOMBS AIR LAUNCHED FROM NORTH SEA AREA
SEPT. 15/16 — NOV. 14/15

Impact sites of the overland air launched flying bombs aimed at London, excluding those shot down by the defences. The grid letters and figures are those in use during the war. Period 15 Sept. to 15 Nov. 1944.

Earlier Phase 2 impact sites. These indicate that a marked decrease in accuracy followed the move from Dutch to German bases. (Crown. Maps in the National Archive files)

A barrage balloon, close hauled but ready to be flown.

As a result of Duncan Sandys's announcement that the battle of London was over many evacuees returned to the capital confident that it was safe. They were just in time to meet both the V2 rocket bombardment and Phase 2 of Operation *Rumpelkammer*, which started on the night of 15/16 September.

General Pile wrote of this time:

> *The great majority of our defences were deployed along the south coast but there was a small additional deployment known as the Diver Gun Box covering the approaches to the capital from the east. Including the normal defences of the area there were 136 static 3.7 inch guns, 210 lighter 40 mm and 410 guns of 20 mm. The latter were manned by the*

navy and the RAF Regiment. There was one Z [anti aircraft] rocket
battery of nine projectors.

We had firm evidence that a new attack from the east was being
launched from aircraft . . . This set us a great problem deciding where
to redeploy the defences of the south-east. The enemy might conceivably
be able to launch attacks simultaneously from the North Foreland to
Yorkshire . . . It was clear that the potential menace was an alarming
one.

Pile's chief, Air Marshal Roderic Hill, recognizing the threat posed
by air-launched flying bombs from the east, authorized the thinning
of the gun belt protecting the south-east to reinforce the gun box in
the quadrangle bounded by Rochester, Whitstable, Clacton and
Chelmsford, thus better protecting the eastern approaches to the
capital, particularly the approach up the Thames Estuary.

They decided not to extend the barrage balloon belt into the area
north of the Thames, since General Pile feared that the balloon
cables would hamper the defence by interfering with the gun
control radar attached to the AA units.

At the beginning of September it was already evident that the
enemy threatened to outflank the gun box with launches aimed at
London from further north across the flat lands of East Anglia. A
more radical reappraisal of defence strategy was already becoming
necessary. On 6 September the Chiefs of Staff proposed that in order
to provide yet more AA equipment for anti-diver use, the area north-
west of a line from the River Humber to the Solent, with specific
exceptions, be stripped of anti-aircraft defences. The Ministry of
Home Security, however, was less than enthusiastic about this.

It was more a matter of location and of having up to date
equipment available than mere numbers of guns. This had been
proved by the redeployment of equipment into the narrow south-
east coastal belt in July against the ramp-launched flies, which was
a great success as it gave the guns complete freedom to shoot down
divers into the sea. Neither the V1s nor the unexploded AA shells
did any harm when they fell into the open sea. The great
improvements in the gunners' performance was due to both the
coastal location and the introduction of revolutionary new
equipment.

Progressively through July and August a new shell fuse, which
had been invented in Britain but developed in the USA, was rushed
into service, and this proved singularly effective against the flying
bomb. Given the code name Bonzo, it operated on a proximity or
variable time principle. The fuse was able to explode a shell in the

optimum position when the round passed near to its target. After firing it began to transmit a signal from a small radio transmitter so that as the shell neared its target the signal echoed. This was sensed by a receiver built into the fuse which then exploded the shell. The straight and level course of the fly as well as its steel bulk assisted this process.

Improved AA radar gun control equipment was also increasingly coming into service. SCR 584 gun-laying radar sets working with number 10 BTL predictors greatly improved the accuracy of the guns. They plotted the flight of the bomb, much assisted by its steady course, speed and height, pointing the gun barrel towards the position where the target would be at the moment when the shell intersected its flight path. The SCR 584 set gave better readings in coastal areas away from the interference which ground contours tended to cause.

It was found during the eighty-day period that night interception of flying bombs could reasonably be undertaken by day fighters if pilots were given night flying training. The divers were self-illuminating to the extent that the pulse-jet flame was visible for miles. The Hawker Tempest fighter was the only British piston-engined aircraft which, without special modification, was able to catch all flying bombs in level flight. The Gloster Meteor jet fighter, which came into action in limited numbers during August against the daylight operations, was not at this stage of its development considered suitable for use against the doodlebugs at night.

It was by no means easy for night-fighter pilots to engage a flying bomb. The difficulties of ranging and aiming against the glare of the pulse jet in the dark were compounded by the propensity of the bomb to explode when shot at. If it was too close the fighter was liable to be damaged, even destroyed, from the blast and debris. If the range was too great the attack was unlikely to be effective.

The day-fighter squadrons used against the V1 in the eighty days became available for reassignment at the beginning of September. The requirement was for two distinct types of night fighter. The first had to be twin engined with a good endurance, and had three roles:

To intercept the air-launch Heinkels

To engage flying bombs between the launching zone and the coastal gun strip

To carry out intruder missions over the bases from which III/KG 3 operated in the hope of catching its aircraft taking off or landing.

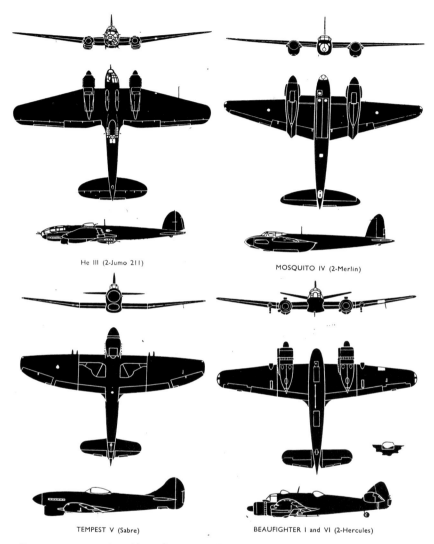

He III (2-Jumo 211)

MOSQUITO IV (2-Merlin)

TEMPEST V (Sabre)

BEAUFIGHTER I and VI (2-Hercules)

Contemporary 1944 identification silhouettes of those aeroplanes taking part in the air-launched flying-bomb battle. (Crown)

Of these the first was considered the most important as its success would sap the morale of the enemy aircrew, minimizing their effectiveness.

The second type of night fighter required was a fast, nimble machine able to catch and shoot down doodlebugs which escaped

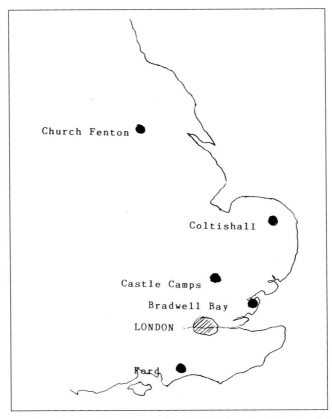

A map showing the location of the airfields involved in the fighter defence of the United Kingdom from the air-launched flying-bomb offensive. (Author)

the coastal anti-aircraft fire. The single-engined Hawker Tempest was selected for this 'long stop' role. No. 501 Squadron equipped with Tempest Mark Vs was posted from Manston airfield in 11 Group area to Bradwell Bay in 12 Group area of Fighter Command on 22 September. To assist it in its night-flying role a detachment of AA searchlights soon followed.

The Mosquito night fighter was judged to be the best to undertake the over-sea and intruder activities. Squadrons equipped with the type were accordingly deployed:

125 Squadron with Mark XVII were posted to Coltishall in Norfolk on 18 October.

25 Squadron with Mark XXX moved from Coltishall to Castle Camps in Cambridgeshire on 27 October.

68 Squadron at Castle Camps in July re-equipped with Mark XVIIs and on 28 October moved to Coltishall.

456 Squadron, equipped with Mark XVIIs, operated out of Ford airfield, Sussex, in the 11 Group area, guarding the southern flank, until it was moved up to Church Fenton in Yorkshire on 31 December.

307 Squadron, equipped with Mark XIIs, operated out of Church Fenton but maintained a detachment at Coltishall. In October it changed its Mosquitos to Mark XXX.

The primary function of 125, 25 and 68 Squadrons was to find and destroy Heinkel carrier planes, but air-launched doodlebugs heading for the coast were also engaged when the opportunity offered. The aircrews had to be very careful not to approach the coastal gun belt at an altitude below 4,000 ft, as the gunners had authority to shoot down all aircraft below that height during the hours of darkness. This rule was to have tragic consequences more than once.

An overlapping chain of CHL radar stations along the East Anglian coast were on constant look-out for low-flying Heinkels and also for incoming flying bombs. Located at Trimley Heath, Bawdsey, Dunwich, Greyfriars, Hopton, Neatishead and Happisburgh, these stations each had a range of about 40 miles. They also had the capacity to distinguish between friendly and enemy plots on their radar screens.

Using this facility, each was able to control an airborne night fighter and guide its crew to within 1½ miles of the target, at which range the aircrew would normally pick up the plot on their airborne interception (AI) radar set. This method was known as ground-control interception (GCI).

The Greyfriars CHL was American-owned and operated. It had a superior range and GCI capacity, but for operational reasons the Americans withdrew their equipment to the Continent in October and it was left to the British to fill the gap.

The ability to distinguish between friendly and hostile plots on the radar screen, identification friend or foe (IFF), took the form of a secondary plot. This derived from special aerials which were linked to an IFF transmitted ('interrogator') and receiver

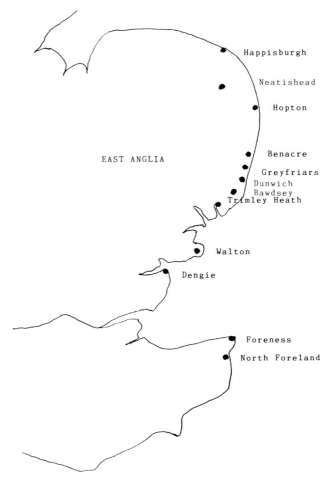

Location of the Chain Home Low and Ground Control Interception radar stations operating against air-launched flying bombs. (Author's map)

('responder'). The IFF transmission passed through a coded transponder in the friendly aircraft, which relayed characteristic identifying pulses. These appeared as secondary traces on the CHL radar screen, which enabled the radar operator to distinguish between the friendly and the apparently hostile plots. Using this information, showing the positions, the radar operator guided the nightfighter towards its target.

Expansion –
Kampfgeschwader 53

As early as 1 December 1943 Adolf Hitler signed a directive activating the LXV Army Corps.

I hereby approve the order issued to LXV Infantry Corps for special employment for the preparation and waging of long-range warfare against England available for this purpose.

Commander-in-Chief, West, is hereby authorized to issue all necessary orders for the preparation and employment of these special weapons to elements of the Luftwaffe, *the Navy, Organization Todt and the* Reichsarbeitsdienst *[Reich Labour Service] stationed in western Europe.*

Generalleutnant Erich Heinmann, an artillery officer, was given command of the new corps. Approximately two-thirds of the HQ staff were army personnel, the others were from the *Luftwaffe.* Heinmann's deputy, *Oberst* Eugen Walter, was a *Luftwaffe* officer and the responsibilities of different sections were divided between the two services, a *Luftwaffe* section head usually having an army deputy and vice versa. Nevertheless the LXV was an army corps, with an army head who had full political backing. It was only to be expected that army tactical thinking would prevail in the use of the V weapons, particularly after the army's own V2 became operational on 8 September.

London was the designated target and the air-launched V1 contribution was directed to this end. With the exception of the four night attacks on Southampton in July, only once was an alternative target raided and that was Manchester in the early hours of

Christmas Eve. This concentration of air-launched effort against a well-defended target amounted to a serious under-utilization of the flexibility of air launching which may be attributed to political direction and, in some measure, effective army control.

By 15 September 1944, III/KG 3 was operational from its German bases and equipped for longer-range attacks. It faced the prospect of rapid expansion as the only means then available to continue the V1 campaign against Britain. A number of factors favoured this expansion, not least the closer proximity to supply depots and the abundance of airfields.

Kampfgeschwader 53, which enjoyed the honorary title of Condor Legion, was withdrawn from the Eastern Front for retraining as the expanded air-launch unit. III/KG 3 was incorporated into it from 15 October 1944 as its nucleus and its I *Gruppe*. Its II *Gruppe* became

Far from the London battle a row of cottages in Tottington, Lancashire, was struck in the early hours of 24 December by a robot aimed at Manchester. Seven people lost their lives here. (Bury Library)

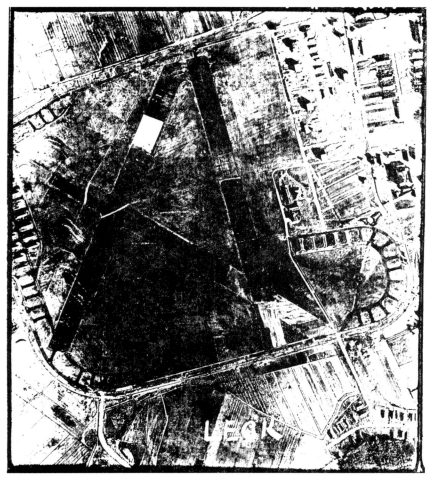

An RAF photoreconnaissance cover of Leck airfield taken on 2 October,
only shortly before the airfield became a base for air-launched VI
operations. (Keele University)

operational on the same day and a III *Gruppe* began its training but
did not join operations until early December.

Heinkel 111 aircraft underwent conversion at Ochatz to equip II
and III *Gruppen*. The old I *Gruppe* was disbanded, its personnel
being distributed between II and III. The *staffeln* were allocated to
separate airfields, as follows:

Airfield	Gruppe of KG 53	Staffel of KG 53
Varelbusch	I	1
Ahlhorn	I	2
Vechta	I	3
Bad Zwischenahn	II	4
This was also the Kampfgeschwader headquarters.		
Jever	II	5
Wittmund	II	6
Leck	III	7
Schleswig	III	8
Eggebek	III	9

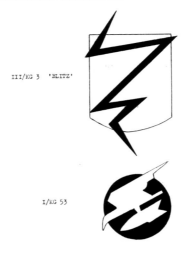

III/KG 3 'BLITZ'

I/KG 53

LEGION CONDOR

II/KG 53

III/KG 53

The Gruppen emblems of the air-launch units engaged in operations. Frank Leyland

Hespepe and Handorf-Munster were also made available to KG 53 as alternative landing grounds for use when the main *staffeln* bases were closed by bad weather of the presence of enemy intruder aircraft.

Weather-reconnaissance flights prior to operations became increasingly important as the winter drew in, and they were carried out for KG 53 by Junkers 88 aircraft of *Wettererkundungsstaffel* 1, which carried the identification code B7.

Hans Hoehler, who qualified as an aircrew wireless operator in mid-October and was then posted to KG 53 has given us an eye-witness account of aircrew training as it was carried on in October and November 1944. Placed in a civilian billet in Zempin on Peenemunde, he waited for a week for his training to begin. It started with a solemn warning of the extreme secrecy surrounding

A Heinkel III H-20u (or H-22) is recognized by its electrically operated dorsal gun turret. With an attached V1, it is being shown to an invited audience. A dark green upper surface is mottled with a light grey to give a seascape effect. The underside appears to be blackened in this case as a night camouflage. In most cases the underside was left in the daylight camouflage of light blue. The bomb is typically painted with a grey/green upper and a pale blue undersurface. (Unknown)

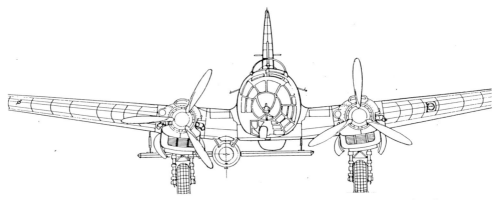

These sketches show the positioning of a loaded operational flying bomb under the starboard wing of a Heinkel carrier. Notice the compressed air link from near the ventral gondola of the Heinkel to the fuselage of the bomb, also the faired-over bomb doors and the steadying arms for the wings of the missile. (Frank Leyland)

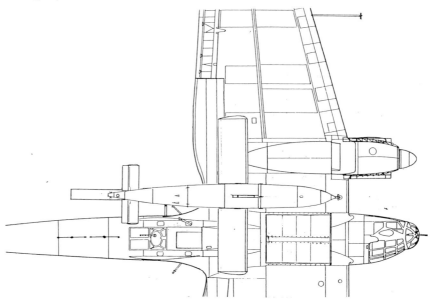

all aspects of the air-launch role, followed by a technical explanation of the workings of the V1. Limitations brought about by the shortage of aviation fuel were already evident so that later in the course, instead of air launching, each crew fired one missile from a ramp under the instruction of Flak Regiment 155 (W) personnel. Hoehler recorded that it was a matter of pride that his crew came nearest to hitting the target, which was moored out in the Baltic Sea. He was given no practical air-launch training before being posted to the third *staffel* of KG 53 at Vechta on 16 November.

A glimpse of the life and methods of operation of the aircrews engaged in air-launching activities from German airfields emerged from the interrogation of the three captured crew members from Heinkel 5K+FS, who were rescued from the sea and landed at Harwich on 8 October. According to the interrogation report crews based at Alhorn were billeted in the village of Grossenkneten some 5 miles from the airfield. The *staffel* captain had an office in the village and all *staffel* life including recreation took place away from the airfield. Dry dinghy drill, for example, was held in the yard of the village inn. Crews were only taken to the airfield at dusk or at night, where they were briefed for the operation. Briefing consisted only of written instructions handed to the observer and wireless operator, together with a talk on the expected weather conditions.

The three prisoners, pilot *Unteroffizer* Klaus Schutz, flight engineer *Unteroffizer* Heinz Webber and air gunner *Obergefreiter* Heinz Muller, proved to be some of the toughest prisoners questioned. Their resistance to interrogation was aided by the absence of the other crew members. *Unteroffizer* Walter Kirchvogel, the wireless operator, was lost in the crash, and *Unteroffizer* Toni Schlich, the observer, drifted away despite their efforts to stay together.

For transporting the doodlebug to its carrier Heinkel and raising it for loading to the aeroplane's bomb pylon a specialist trolley was constructed. This consisted of a lightweight tractor and a hydraulically operated fork lift on a trailer. Made by the Scheusch firm in Erurt, the two pieces of equipment were sometimes combined as in the version shown here. The equipment was also put to other uses as in handling the Messerschmitt 163 rocket propelled fighter. (Frank Leyland)

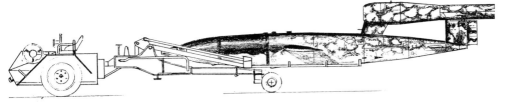

At Vechta airfield armourers fit the wings of a V1 still on its storage dolly. The top camouflage finish of the bomb looks untidy. A hoist is clamped to the T-section lifting lug above the centre of gravity of the missile. (Hans Lachler)

Heinkel III H-16u (W.Nr 161600) A1+HK of 2/KG 53 at Ahlhorn airfield. The 'u' signifies a modified example, in this case adapted to launch a flying bomb. The dorsal gun position identifies this mark, as does the works numbering. The tube sticking out from the side of the Heinkel fuselage projects the looped cable linking the power supply in the aircraft to the sparking plug on the top of the pulse-jet tube on the missile. (Hans Lachler)

Mounted on a **scheuschlepper**, *a tricycle-wheeled trolley with hand-pumped hydraulic lifting arms, this V1 is being moved into position beneath the starboard wing root of a Heinkel III. A protective cone over the nose of the weapon remains in position to guard its air-log propeller from damage. The bomber still has its canvas nose cover in place. (Hans Lachler)*

A close-up of a V1 suspended from its carrier aircraft. The starboard wing of the missile is nearly behind the undercarriage leg of the plane. The wings had to be removed and refitted to facilitate loading to the aeroplane. The individual identification letter of the Heinkel B stands alone on its fuselage side, the other identification letters being omitted for security reasons – 1K+BT. (Hans Lachler)

The crew joined 8 *Staffel* of III/KG 3, soon to become 2 *Staffel* of KG 53, in the middle of September and gathered from longer-serving members of the unit that it had previously been in northern France and latterly at Venlo. Several of the seven or eight crews already in the *staffel* had previous torpedo-dropping experience.

They claimed that at the start of the operation the loaded Heinkel awaited them at the end of the runway ready for take-off, and after the mission they were taken straight back to their billets. The flying bomb itself was covered with a net which was only removed after the crew had boarded the aircraft. The wireless operator, however, had noticed that a metal tube connected the aircraft to the port side of the bomb. When shown a sectional drawing of the Heinkel III the pilot estimated that the point of suspension was under the rearmost of the two main wing spars. No part of the missile, he said, could be seen from the pilot's position.

The flight engineer was familiar with the *zahlwerk* apparatus, which he knew by name, and had been instructed in the method of release of the flying bomb. The instrument was contained in a box placed slightly above and in front of the pilot and observer; the front panel of the box was 20 cm high and 10–12 cm wide, with a lighted centre panel with illuminated digits. The box and digits were duplicated in the flight engineer's position, with the addition of a red and a black button to the right of the box and a lever beneath for the release of the bomb. The observer supplemented the readings on the box by telling the flight engineer when to press the button. The black button, known as the *anstellknopf*, was for starting up the power unit of the flying bomb, whilst the red button, known as the *abstellknopf*, was for stopping the propulsion unit if necessary.

Once the *zahlwerk* had been started the observer only had to wait until the figure 1,000 appeared, at which point the pilot was instructed to begin his climb to launch height. When 100 appeared he instructed the flight engineer to get ready, then to start up the missile power unit and finally to release the bomb. Both the pilot and the flight engineer had an emergency release lever available to enable the bomb to be jettisoned should the need arise.

The prisoners convinced their interrogators that their knowledge was very incomplete, mainly owing to the thorough security. Critically, they concealed, or were unaware of, the vital information, that relating to the *Zyclops* transmitters and navigational system on which Phase 2 of the air-launch campaign depended.

In early March 1945, after the cessation of air-launch operations, a prisoner was interrogated who was said to have served in a

In the armourer's hangar the fuelled and preset robot has been hoisted onto a scheuschlepper *and is ready for towing to its assigned Heinkel.* (Hans Lachler)

'responsible capacity' on the ground staff of 9/KG 53 when it was engaged in air-launching activities. The prisoner, who was described as 'observant and apparently truthful', gave an account which went a long way towards filling the gaps and correcting some of the misinformation relating to the life and activities of a typical KG 53 *staffel*. He said that KG 53 was withdrawn to the Reich in September 1944 after two years on the Russian front.

He made the remarkable claim that in mid-December II *Gruppe* lost twelve of its Heinkels owing to premature detonation of flying bombs shortly after take-off and that this resulted in the *gruppe* losing operational status for a fortnight. However false this is in relation to KG 53, this may have happened earlier to III/KG 3.

Fuelled and prepared, the V1 on its scheuschlepper *is towed away. The loaded* scheuschlepper *tended to be tail heavy so that the weight of the armourers riding on the front end helped to keep it balanced in transit.* (Hans Lachler)

He described the preparations made for operations, saying that on the afternoon preceding a raid, the flying bombs needed were brought from storage dispersal to the servicing hangar by field railway. After fuelling and preparation by specialized armourers, the flying bombs were taken to and slung under the carrier Heinkels on an apron outside the servicing hangar. The loaded aircraft were then towed back to dispersal, where they were themselves fuelled.

According to his account two *gruppen* were operational by mid-October with a total strength of sixty aircraft and crews. By

December a serious aviation fuel shortage was hampering operations and no fuel stocks were held at airfields. No. 9 *Staffel*, he said, had eighteen or twenty Heinkels and sixteen or seventeen crews. Up to the end of December it had suffered no casualties.

The prisoner described and drew a sketch map of the airfield at Eggebeck used by 9 *Staffel*. This was a former fighter school which had a new hangar erected for the use of KG 53.

The V1 stock arrived by train to be dispersed and camouflaged near the airfield. A new taxi track enabled the Heinkels to be dispersed along the southern fringe of woodland, in earth blast pens under camouflage netting. New huts were erected in the woods for the armourers. Some Arado training aircraft were parked in the old north-western dispersal area to mislead Allied air reconnaissance. The flying personnel of the unit were accommodated in the village of Bollingstedt, some 7 km from the airfield.

With wings removed, the diver is manoeuvred into position under the bomb-carrier pylon beneath the starboard wing of the aeroplane. The protective cone covering the nose of the missile has now been removed. The front steadier buffers against which the nose of the missile will rest are clearly seen. The hydraulic arms of the scheuschlepper *on which the bomb rests will be pumped upwards until the T-shaped lug on top of the missile engages with the suspension point under the bomb-carrying pylon.* (Hans Lachler)

Heinkel III H-16u, A1+HL of 3/KG53 stands loaded with its bomb. The engines are fitted with flame dampers over the exhaust stacks in an attempt to conceal the flame a glare in the dark. No bomb sight or front armament is fitted. Where the nose gun position is faired over the individual aircraft identification letter H appears. The light blue underside of the aircraft and missile are typical since the low altitude at which the operations took place over the sea made black camouflage paint unnecessary. The verti* part of the pipe connecting a compressed air supply carried in the aircraft to start up t V1 is just visible beyond the forehead of the bending airman.* (Hans Lachler)

Heinkel III H-20 A1+GA stands ready for operation, providing a good view of some armament, an Mg 131z in the turret and a twin Mg 81 in the beam mounting abov the cable tube to the V1. The individual aircraft identification letter G is evident on the side of th fuselage amongst the mottled grey and green camouflage. (Hans Lachler)

He named the leading personalities of KG 53 known to him:

Geschwader Kommodore:	*Oberst Leutnant* Pochrandt
Technical Officer:	*Hauptmann* Kindt
III *Gruppe Kommandeur*:	Major Almendinger
Technical Officer:	*Hauptmann* Neidhardt
Staffelkapitan 7/KG 53:	*Oberleutnant* Laurer
Staffelkapitan 8/KG 53:	*Oberleutnant* Dengg
Staffelkapitan 9/KG 53:	*Hauptmann* Jessen

The pilots of 9 *Staffel* were *Hauptmann* Ebner, *Oberleutnant* Neuhaus, *Oberleutnant* Antz, *Leutnant* Masterleck, *Leutnant* Goldbeck, *Leutnant* Bartsch, *Leutnant* Penneckdorf, *Leutnant* Butzer, *Leutnant* Kemk, *Leutnant* Eisenschmidt, *Stabsfeldwebel* Schimpf, *Feldwebel* Kaiser, *Fahnenjunker Feldwebel* Sonntag, *Feldwebel* Schulze.

It was not until April 1945 that an air-launch equipped Heinkel was captured and available for Allied examination. Whilst much of its equipment was stripped out and sent to Britain for evaluation, the matter was by then no longer of any pressing importance.

CHAPTER SIX

September – All
Strafe London

On 15 September 1944, with the V2 rocket bombardment of London proceeding, III/KG 3 became operational from its German bases, equipped with and instructed in the use of its *Zyclops-zahlwerk* navigational system.

Phase 2 of the air-launched flying-bomb campaign commenced that night.

The night of 15/16 September
There was thick cloud and rain over the North Sea, with a cloud base between 600 and 1200 ft. A 25 mph wind blew from the south-east. It was the first night after a new moon.

All three *staffel* captains of III/KG 3 were briefed at *gruppe* HQ for this operation and they in turn briefed their own operational crews at their respective airfields. The aircraft of individual *staffeln* took off at five-minute intervals and made for the Den Helder beacon, from whence the *zahlwerk* settings entered by the navigators would commence count-down to the missile-release point.

Fifteen Heinkels made launches over the period 05.35–06.00 hours. Seven of these launches failed, the missiles plunging into the sea immediately or at least before reaching the coast. Two were shot down by naval gunners probably stationed in the port of Felixstowe defences. Two more were shot down by a Tempest night fighter of 501 Squadron piloted by an American airman serving with the RAF, Flying Officer B.F. Miller. He reported that he was scrambled from Bradwell Bay airfield under Trimley ground control radar guidance to deal with divers coming in north of Felixstowe.

Having moved its bases from Holland to north-west Germany, III/KG 3 reopened the air-launched flying-bomb campaign on the night of 15/16 September. Just before dawn one missile fell with devastating effect at St Awdry's Road, Barking, London, as shown in these two views. Thirteen people were reported killed here and over a hundred were injured. (US Army Signal Corps.)

I climbed to 7,000 ft and saw a diver coming in on a course of 285 degrees at 2,500 ft and 340 mph. I dived down on it and closed in from 500 yards astern then opened fire. I saw strikes on the tail unit. Control told me to break off the engagement and I did so. I saw the diver losing height, crash and explode on the ground near RAF Castle Camps airfield 30 seconds after my attack at 06.06 hours.

I saw a second one at 06.08 heading over Bradwell Bay on a course of 250 degrees at 340 mph. I closed in astern and opened fire from 500 yards closing to 50 yards. The diver blew up in mid air.

The two flies shot down by Flying Officer Miller ended their flights at Felsted, 8 miles north of Chelmsford and at Saffron Walden. The others fell at:

> Barking, London, at 05.52 hours. After an alert at 05.49 a doodlebug made a direct hit on houses at St Awdry's Road, close to its junction with Ripple Road. Five of the two-storey terraced houses were destroyed and another two severely damaged. Thirteen people were killed and seventeen seriously injured in this incident.
>
> Woolwich, London, at 05.59 hours. This missile fell on the foreshore of the Thames near Long's Wharf at the junction of Warspite Road and Harrington Road. A barge was sunk and there was blast damage to wharf buildings. The crater was filled with river water.
>
> Latchington, Essex, 12 miles east-south-east of Chelmsford, at 06.14 hours.
>
> St Margaret's at Cliffe, Kent. This fell close inshore, causing some blast damage.

The night of 17/18 September

The nights were getting longer; sunset was at 19.11 hours. Only six aircraft launched, between 20.30 and 20.45 hours. Three launches were abortive.

The *Daily Herald* of 18 September reported this attack under the heading '*Flying Bombs Over – A Small Number of Divers*'. Censorship precluded the publication of any detailed information.

The following incidents were recorded:

> Canewdon, Essex, 7 miles north of Southend, at 20.40 hours. This fly fell to AA fire.
>
> Thorpe Bay, Essex, between Southend and Shoeburyness, at 20.47 hours.
>
> St Marylebone, London, at 20.50 hours. After an alert at 20.47

hours the missile fell some 300 ft north of the boathouse in Regent's Park. There was a crater 20 × 5 ft but trees took the main force of the blast.

The night of 18/19 September

In the early hours of Tuesday, 19 September some of the residents of the Lincolnshire seaside town of Skegness heard the rattle, sometimes described as similar to the sound of a badly tuned motorcycle engine, of a V1 passing over the town from east to west. It literally broke new ground when it exploded in a potato field at Tan Vats near Metheringham, 8 miles south-east of Lincoln. Whether this bomb was deliberately aimed here or was the result of a technical or navigational fault is unknown. Direction of flight suggests that the launch was from a point well to the north of the relatively narrow launch zone otherwise used.

Twelve launches took place this time, between 04.00 and 04.30 hours, four of which were abortive. The following incidents occurred:

Toppersfield, Essex, 6 miles north-east of Halstead, at 04.10 hours.
Tan Vats, Lincolnshire, at 04.20 hours.
Mitcham, London, also at 04.20 hours. After an alert at 04.15 hours there was a direct hit on houses on the west side of Avenue Road, near its junction with Northborough Road. Fourteen terraced two-storey houses were wrecked and another ten severely damaged.
Tollesbury, Essex, 21 miles east of Maldon, at 04.33 hours.
Hornchurch, Essex, 14 miles east-north-east of central London, also at 04.33 hours. This robot killed four people and injured twenty-nine when it struck Crystal Avenue.
Hornchurch, Essex, at 04.40 hours. A second missile killed ten people and injured thirty-eight. It demolished six houses and seriously damaged fifty when it fell at Llewyns Lane. Some 600 houses suffered minor damage.
Romford, Essex.
Battlesbridge, Essex, 8 miles north-west of Southend.

Three divers were reported to have flown east to west over Felixstowe between 04.11 and 04.25 hours.

George Beardmore, the writer, who lived in North Harrow, London, brought his family home from evacuation on 19 September and recorded in his diary: 'Fly bombs have resumed. We have been entreated by the Government to leave mothers and children in the country but Jean loves her home too much to obey.'

The night of 19/20 September
Fifteen Heinkels launched between about 01.30 and 01.50 hours. Possibly because of a miscalculation in the forecast wind strength, all but one of the missiles which crossed the coast fell to the north of London. Seven launches were aborted, one bomb was shot down by AA over land and seven evaded the defences. Those that landed were as follows:

> Little Baddow, Essex, 4 miles east of Chelmsford, at 01.45 hours. This diver fell at Duke's Orchard House, which was partially demolished, and fifty other properties were damaged. Mrs Gregory Nicholson, the Secretary of the Essex Drama League, was killed and two other people seriously injured.
> Rushden, Hertfordshire, 5 miles east of Letchworth, at 01.50 hours.
> Lawford, Essex, 6 miles north-east of Colchester, also at 01.50 hours.
> Great Dunmow, Essex, 14 miles north-east of Chelmsford, also at 01.50 hours.
> Bethnal Green, London, at 01.52 hours. This bug hit the east side of Cambridge Heath Road near its junction with Roman Road. Severe damage was done to nine houses.
> Essendon, Hertfordshire, 3 miles east of Hatfield, at 02.10 hours.
> Cockfield, Suffolk, 7 miles south-south-east of Bury St Edmunds, also at 02.10 hours.
> Maldon, Essex. Damaged by AA fire this missile flew into a hill in the town where it destroyed a number of houses. There were twelve casualties including one couple rescued injured from a Morrison indoor shelter.

The enemy too took casualties this time. Two Heinkels, possibly *en route* to Den Helder, collided and crashed at Gaastmeer Scharl, Friesland, in Holland. Four crew members baled out successfully but six were killed, including the *staffel* commander of 8 *Staffel*, *Oberleutnant* Bohnet.

The night of 20/21 September
Two separate attacks were launched this night, the first between 20.53 and 21.25 hours, the second between 04.10 and 04.25 hours.

A multiple attack had the effect of causing maximum harassment of the civilian population and also put extra strain on the defenders by extending the period of standing to and fighter patrols. As the Heinkels launched over a relatively short period only a small number of fighters could be in the right place at the right time. Of the nineteen launched, eight were aborted, one was shot down by AA over the sea and one over land. Those that got through in the first attack fell as follows:

Chediston, Suffolk, 9 miles west of Southwold, at 20.48 hours. The diver impacted in a field 120 yards east of Grove Farm doing considerable damage to the buildings. Four stacks were burned down and agricultural machinery destroyed. The serial number of the bomb, 701422, as found stencilled on one of its fragments. Fortunately there were no casualties.

Richmond Park, London, at 20.54 hours. A potentially well-aimed shot impacted between Pond and Hamcross Plantation. Apart from a crater 16 × 3 ft no significant damage resulted.

Poplar, London, at 21.00 hours. This V1 fell into the Thames at West India Dock but only destroyed two light wooden structures and a single-storey brick building used as a store by the NFS.

Codicote, Hertfordshire, 4 miles south-south-east of Stevenage, at 21.15 hours.

Wandsworth, London, at 21.25 hours. This fell in a garden alongside 8 Lebanon Road, wrecking five semi-detached houses and seriously damaging another seven. It was noticed that an Anderson shelter on the edge of the crater remained intact, although no mention was made of any occupants.

Waltham Holy Cross, London, at 21.33 hours. This exploded in trees beside allotments on the east bank of Cobbins Brook on the south side of Honey Lane. No significant damage resulted.

The accuracy achieved in the first attack was lacking in the second. Bombs fell as follows:

Great Totham, Essex, 12 miles south-west of Colchester, at 04.25 hours.

Felixstowe, Suffolk, at 04.27 hours. The fly approached from the north-east and fell below the high-water mark on the beach 3½ miles north-east of the town. It was probably first damaged by AA fire.

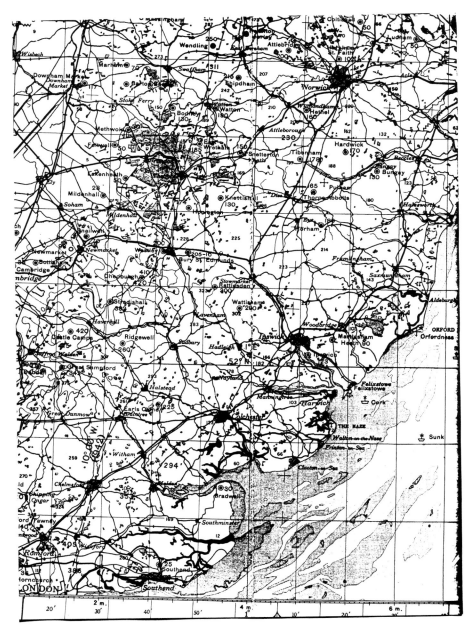

The north-eastern approaches to London as they appear on an RAF flying map of 1944. (Crown)

GM·182-1-467)(26-9-44)("BUZZ"BOMB - 145)

Wreckage from the V1 that fell on 24 September at Swainsthorpe in Norfolk. It was collected by the USAAF who photographed it on the 26th.

Near Hatfield, Hertfordshire, at 04.35 hours.
Hacheston, Suffolk, 14 miles north-east of Ipswich, at 04.40 hours. Three houses were damaged and a girl was slightly injured when the missile exploded in a field north-east of Bridge Farm. The serial number of the bomb was 701427.

The night of 22/23 September
Twelve Heinkels from 8 and 9 *Staffeln* launched an attack between about 20.20 and 20.40 hours, but it was not to be a successful night's work for some seven out of twelve of the flying bombs failed after launch, and only one reached London. One was shot down by AA over the sea, and one over land. The other two fell short of the capital. The incidents were as follows:

Bradwell, Essex, 12 miles south of Colchester, at 20.35 hours. This was the diver that fell to AA fire.

Enfield, London, at 20.40 hours. A field was cratered 240 yards west-south-west of the junction between Enfield Road and Cotswold Avenue. Adjoining property was damaged.

Little Heath, Hertfordshire, 4 miles west-north-west of Hemel Hempstead, also at 20.40 hours.

Near Hatfield, Hertfordshire, at 20.50 hours.

The night of 23/24 September

Two separate raids occurred again, the second being of shorter duration. They involved fifteen carriers. The first attack lasted from 21.20 to 21.55 hours and the second from 04.35 to 04.50 hours. All the bombs recorded on land were plotted north of the London area, one falling as far away as Norfolk. Seven were abortive, one was shot down by a fighter over the sea and one by AA over land. Six got through.

Handorf Bei Minster airfield was attacked on that night by over 100 Lancasters of Bomber Command and it was reported that 7 *Staffel* of KG 3 lost four aircraft as a result.

The incidents in the first attack were at:

Thaxted, Essex, 17 miles north-north-west of Chelmsford, at 21.40 hours.

Braughing, Hertfordshire, 9 miles south-south-west of Letchworth, at 21.49 hours.

In the second attack the following places were hit:

Swainsthorpe, Norfolk, 5 miles south of Norwich, at 04.42 hours. The LNER railway line was blocked 200 yards north of Brick Kiln Yard by trees which were blown down. Windows were broken both here and in neighbouring Poringland.

Framsden, Suffolk, 9 miles east of Stowmarket, at 04.45 hours. The diver exploded 450 yards north of the aptly named Blastings Farm. Damage was done to three houses and to barns but there were no casualties.

Codicote, Hertfordshire, 4 miles north-north-west of Welwyn.

Pirton, Hertfordshire, 3 miles west of Letchworth.

Burwell, Cambridgeshire, 4 miles north-east of Newmarket.

The doodlebug shot down over the sea was credited to Flight Lieutenant J.S. Limbert and Flying Officer H.S. Cook flying Mosquito HK 300 of 25 Squadron. It may have cost the Mosquito crew their lives, for they did not return from their patrol and were posted as missing 'believed to be attacking a flying bomb'.

The night of 24/25 September
This was a rainy night with a cloud base of between 600 and 700 ft. Sixteen aircraft launched V1s, again spread over two separate attacks. The first took place between 21.30 and 22.40 hours, the second, which was the better directed of the two, between 04.40 and 05.15 hours. Eleven bombs were abortive, and one was shot down by a fighter over land. Four got through. Hits in the first attack were:

Hessett, Suffolk, 5 miles east of Bury St Edmunds, at 22.00 hours.
Tilbury Juxta St Clare, Essex, 12 miles north of Braintree, at 22.05 hours.
Chertsey, Surrey, on the Thames west of London, at 22.50 hours.

In the second attack, incidents were as follows:

Enfield, London, at 05.17 hours. A field was cratered 300 yards north of Holly Hill Farm, Ridgeway. Damage was done to the farm buildings.
Chigwell, London, at 05.29 hours. The missile, reported to have been shot down by Flying Officer B.F. Miller of 501 Squadron, impacted in allotments north of Alderton Way, Loughton. A footbridge over the LNER railway line was damaged.

Thick cloud over the Dutch coast frustrated Wing Commander L.J. Mitchell and Flight Lieutenant D.L. Cox of 25 Squadron in Mosquito HK 357. They obtained a visual sighting of a Heinkel and fired into it, observing strikes on the starboard wing root but the target escaped at 1,000 ft.

The night of 25/26 September
This turned out to be another night of poor performances by III/KG 3. Ten aircraft attacked between 22.40 and 22.55 hours. Six bombs were abortive, two were shot down by AA over the sea and one over land. Only one evaded defences and fell at Bacon's Farm, Henham, Essex, at 23.00 hours. Two people were slightly injured and three houses were rendered uninhabitable. The one that fell to the AA gunners landed at Great Bromley, Essex, 4 miles east of Colchester, at 23.03 hours.

The night of 26/27 September

A small operation the following night met with little more success. Seven launchings were made between 03.39 and 03.45 hours, of which only two got through. Two were shot down by AA over land. The incidents were at:

The barrage balloon shield established to the south of London during the ramp-launched main V1 offensive was extended up to the River Thames during the air-launched phase, but no farther. One air-launched doodlebug is thought to have been caught by a balloon cable on 8 October and this photograph of damage done at Fawkham Green with a lowered balloon in the background appears to bear this out. (Kent Messenger Newspapers)

Sible Hedingham, Essex, 8 miles south-west of Sudbury, at 03.45 hours.

Ardleigh, Essex, 4 miles north-east of Colchester, at 03.50 hours. Four people were killed here – Mrs Ada Cheeseman, her two children and Mr Wilfred Jaggard, aged seventy. The missile was damaged by AA fire and apparently glided down, for one witness described its descent as sounding like a 'whistling bomb', probably due to the escape of compressed air within its body.

Edmonton, London, at 03.53 hours. After an alert at 03.50 hours, one of the evaders impacted in the rear garden of a house on the south side of Woodgrange Gardens. It made a crater 14 × 5 ft only a few yards north-east of the junction with Woodgate Road, amongst two-storeyed terraced dwellings. Two homes were totally destroyed, three severely damaged and nine others suffered lesser damage. An Anderson shelter only 10 ft from the crater was demolished. Twenty-five people were injured, eleven of them seriously.

Maldon, Essex, at 03.55 hours. After being hit by AA fire one fell in open farmland in the parish of St Lawrence.

The *Essex County Standard* of 29 September gave a graphic, if guarded, account of the Ardleigh incident:

The first fatal casualties from flying bombs in one area of Southern England were caused in the early hours of Wednesday morning when one of the robots crashed on a row of cottages, doing damage to civilian property. Four thatched cottages were totally destroyed, another group were rendered uninhabitable and two brick houses were badly damaged.

All the thatched cottages caught fire immediately and it was not long before they were destroyed. Mr Herbert Bacon, 64 and Mr Frederick Pitt, 45, it is understood, were indoors looking out of the windows when the blast broke the panes. They were badly cut about the face and were later admitted to hospital. Theirs were amongst the homes destroyed.

Other houses were damaged. The whole side of one was blown off. A farmhouse lost practically all the tiles from its roof. The body of the house was saved by a barn standing in front which took most of the blast and was badly damaged.

One man, living in a house down the road, who had built a concrete shelter for his family at the beginning of the war, heard the gliding bomb and thought it had passed over before he heard the crash. He made good use of the shelter, and even though the door was on the opposite side from the blast, the jamb was wrenched from its fittings. His house was damaged, the tiles being loosened and torn off. Some of the windows were broken. The blast pulled down the curtains and several shelves of his shed, which he used for a workshop.

Throughout the day rescue workers and firemen were engaged in clearing up the devastated area. Hoses were still being played on the smoking rubble in the afternoon and GPO workers were repairing damage to telephone wires.

The night of 28/29 September

There was broken cloud between 1,200 and 2,000 ft with a haze below, satisfactory weather for air launching. Between 05.00 and 05.50 hours eleven Heinkels attacked, of which four were abortive. Overland missiles fell as follows:

Chelmondiston, Suffolk, between Felixstowe and Ipswich, at 05.07 hours. Damaged by AA fire, the robot exploded on hitting trees in Bylam Wood, damaging two nearby houses.

Saffron Walden, Essex, at 05.20 hours. This V1 fell in the parish of Littlebury.

Barrow, Suffolk, 5 miles west of Bury St Edmunds, at 05.23 hours.

Edwardstone, Suffolk, 14 miles west of Ipswich, at 05.30 hours.

Barnston, Essex, near Dunmow, at 05.45 hours. Flight Lieutenant R.J. Lilwall, patrolling in a 501 Squadron Tempest, saw a fly coming towards him at 250 mph and 500 ft. Closing, he fired five short bursts at it. On the last of these he saw ammunition strikes as he overshot the target, climbing. It exploded below and slightly behind him without reaching the ground.

Bygrave, Hertfordshire, in a rural setting 4 miles north-east of Letchworth, at 06.00 hours.

Sutton, Cambridgeshire, 12 miles north of Cambridge.

Radio intercepts indicated that at least one aircraft of 8 *Staffel* was involved in the raid.

It proved to be an expensive night for III/KG 3. Wing Commander L.J. Mitchell and Flight Lieutenant D.L. Cox, flying a Mosquito of 25 Squadron, claimed two Heinkels destroyed over the sea between 05.20 and 05.45 hours.

The night of 29/30 September

The last raid of September was a larger-scale affair, involving a double attack extending over the periods 20.40–21.30 hours and 04.10–04.30 hours.

The first attack was the heavier of the two but suffered the greater number of failed launches. A plot of the impact sites shows a wide scatter, with incidents both north and south of London.

Flying Officer Travers, piloting a Mosquito XXX of 25 Squadron on an anti-diver patrol over the North Sea, reported that he spotted one flying bomb over the sea but on closing found that it had 'gone haywire' and was orbiting and climbing. The appearance of a suspicious aircraft behind Travers ended his enjoyment of its antics. The total number of abortive launches was eleven. Three bombs were shot down by AA, one over the sea and two over land, leaving just six that evaded the defences.

The first attack resulted in three incidents:

Baythorpe End, Essex, 4 miles south-east of Haverhill, at 20.45 hours.

Walthamstow, London, at 21.36 hours. Following an alert at 21.33 hours a V1 struck the south side of Forest Road, just east of its junction with Gaywood Road. It fell amongst two-storeyed terraced dwellings and shops with dwellings above. Twelve of these were destroyed and two more severely damaged.

Shudy Camps, Cambridgeshire, 3 miles west of Haverhill.

In the second attack, the following incidents were recorded:

Wixoe, Suffolk, 5 miles east of Castle Camps airfield, at 04.22 hours.

Tiptree, Essex, 8 miles south-west of Colchester, at 04.23 hours. This diver fell to AA fire.

Nazeing, Essex, 4 miles south-west of Harlow, at 04.37 hours. This was the first air-launched flying bomb to come down in Britain without exploding. An examination revealed an interesting variation in operational practice, it was found that detonators had not been fitted to activate the spoilers under the tailplane. These detonators normally terminated the flight of the doodlebug at its preset range. Their omission explained the sometimes long glide with which missiles terminated their flights. The range in these cases was determined only by the amount of fuel carried.

Meopham, Kent, 6 miles west of Chatham, at 04.37 hours. Ten people were injured when this bug was shot down by AA. It destroyed farm buildings and did extensive damage to cottages.

Rudgwick, Sussex, 5 miles west-north-west of Horsham, at 04.40 hours.

CHAPTER SEVEN

October – Rising Pressure

In more favourable conditions, III/KG 3 resumed the campaign after a pause of several days – probably caused by a period of full moon. The heaviest attacks were reserved where possible for clear nights with little or no moon.

The night of 5/6 October

Broken cloud from a base of about 2,000 ft provided some cover in otherwise good visibility. Eleven Heinkels attacked after moonset, between 19.40 and 20.00 hours. A twelfth crew was briefed to take part but Heinkel 111 coded 5K+FS of 8/KG 3 came down in the sea about 50 miles off Yarmouth with engine trouble. Three of its crew were landed as prisoners at Harwich. Only one of the eleven attacks was abortive, but five were shot down, one over the sea.

Incidents recorded were:

Stutton, Suffolk, 5 miles south of Ipswich, at 19.53 hours. Mrs Louisa Phillis, a widow aged sixty-six was seriously injured and another person slightly injured when a V1, damaged by AA fire, fell on a hedgerow just west of Holly Farm. The farm was severely damaged and five houses were also affected.

Sheering, Essex, 5 miles south of Bishops Stortford, at 19.55 hours. This was another score for the AA gunners.

Romford, Essex at 19.58 hours. Flying Officer J.A. Johnson, a Canadian serving with 501 Squadron, patrolling in Tempest SD-K accounted for this one.

Surbiton, London, at 20.03 hours. Two people were killed as a result of a direct hit on a two-storeyed, semi-detached brick house on the north side of Derby Road. It was destroyed and another seven houses seriously damaged. Burning petrol from a garaged motor car caused a small fire.

Colchester, Essex, at 20.04 hours. Hit by AA, this robot turned over and hurtled down to explode near Reed Hall. A remarkable escape was experienced by soldiers who were in a hut in the direct line of flight of the weapon. Convenient trees intercepted its course and it exploded near some football pitches. There were many casualties from flying glass and one man had his arm broken. Houses had windows blown out and the ceilings of two were damaged by blast. A householder described the road as a mass of flames and said that it was a miracle that the houses escaped; most of them had doors blown off. But for the trees the damage could well have been worse. All that remained at the impact centre were the charred trunks of two trees. Parts of the bomb were found with AA shell damage.

Leatherhead, Surrey, at 20.07 hours

Edgware, London, also at 20.07 hours

Heston, London, at 20.10 hours. This hit the rear garden of 25 Summerhouse Avenue amongst two-storeyed semi-detached dwellings. It caused injuries to fifteen people. An outbreak of fire was caused when petrol in a garaged car ignited.

Chertsey, Surrey, west of central London, at 20.15 hours. Six people were killed here.

The writer George Beardmore recorded something of the aftermath of the Edgware incident. The explosion interrupted the tenor of his life for a while when 14 and 16 Methuen Road, Canon's Park were torn apart. Six other houses were also wrecked, all of them two-storeyed, semi-detached houses. Seventy-four in total were rendered uninhabitable. Five people were killed and forty injured.

Beardmore's account of the far-reaching consequences of the incident is in many ways representative.

The Womens Voluntary Service and I manned the office on the [incident] site for four days with credit to the WVS.

One of the notable incidents was our endeavour to trace the natural son of a man who, with his wife, was numbered amongst the five [people killed]. Apparently he had been a bad lot, for none of the legitimate issue and relatives would say much about him. His half-brother, a naval lieutenant, would not admit to the missing man's existence but instead maintained that he had no brother, which contradicted what the local postman had to say.

However it was my business to find the half-brother, if he still existed. I traced his 1939 employers, ascertaining that he was in the Corps of Military Police. The CMP Records Office could not identify him as theirs, presumably because he was using another name. Eventually he was traced by the CMP, even though he had never been one of their members, to the Green Howards and to temporary residence in the 'Glasshouse' at Aldershot. It is nice to be able to report that he was released for the funeral in the care of a CMP corporal and stood beside his naval half-brother at the graveside.

The phenomenon of bomb happiness appeared in the form of a man with blood stains down his shirt and joy all over his face. He could not stop talking. He said, 'I have lost everything. Suddenly – Bang – just like that. I cannot even find my wife. Nobody seems to know, would you believe it? Ration books, marriage certificate, my father's letters to my mother, kids' birth certificates – the whole lot. Well, I mean, what can I do? – we were asleep. I have come to ask you if you know where Christine is . . . ' and so on, waving his arms about and appealing to the audience between laughs.

Told his wife and little girl were in hospital, neither of them seriously injured, he went off to see them, just as he was, before anyone could stop him.

The enemy too suffered a punishing night. In addition to the aircraft lost off Yarmouth, a Heinkel crashed near Vrouwenzand, Friesland, but the crew survived. Two other carriers were lost through a collision at Nijerirdum-Kippenburg, possibly *en route* to the Den Helder radio beacon. All ten of the crew were killed.

No. 25 Squadron flew seven anti-air-launch patrols, during one of which Flight Lieutenant J.R.F. Jones and Flying Officer R. Skinner, flying Mosquito XVII HK 239 claimed a Heinkel. Under Greyfriars control they obtained an airborne radar contact to starboard and below them. They turned and closed in a stern chase. At 800 yards they saw the target release a V1 and obtained a visual sighting on a Heinkel 111 against a dark sky. The target began to weave and lose height. The Mosquito opened fire from 800 ft and again from 600 ft, striking the fuselage and starboard wing root before overshooting the enemy at 160 mph. The crew saw a large fire on the water at the position of last contact, the time being 19.45 hours.

The night of 6/7 October

The weather proved favourable this night, with thick cloud cover and rain over the North Sea, but otherwise fair visibility. Aircraft of III/KG 3 were involved in a fairly accurate attack between 19.40 and 20.25 hours. Two of the three flies which evaded the defences fell in the London area. Five were shot down and four were abortive. Two of the five shot down landed in the sea, one as a result of action by a fighter. It fell without a shot being fired at it. Flight Lieutenant H. Humphreys and Pilot Officer P. Robertson of 68 Squadron got ahead of it close enough for their slipstream to upset the gyroscopic system and the missile fell out of control.

At 19.31 hours 25 Squadron enjoyed a greater success. Flight Lieutenant E.E. Marshall and Flying Officer C.A. Allen, flying Mosquito XVII HK 257 caught up with a Heinkel and, according to their report, 'blew it to pieces'.

The following incidents were recorded:

Woodhouse Ferrers, Essex, in the Chelmsford rural district, at 19.55 hours. Shot down by Flying Officer R.C. Deleuze of 501 Squadron, this was an air burst.

The censor quartered this photograph, allowing only the unrecognizable bottom left to be published. The incident happened at 20.07 on the evening of Friday, 6 October, when an air-launched robot found its mark in the heart of London's City, striking business premises in Old Jewry near its junction with Gresham Street. (Unknown)

Orpington, London, at 20.06 hours. After an alert at 20.04 hours a doodlebug exploded in trees on a hillside east of Hangrove Hill, doing blast damage to cottages.

City of London, at 20.07 hours. A diver fell on the west side of Old Jewry, south of its junction with Gresham Street. Severe damage was done to four-storeyed, terraced brick-built business premises. Fire broke out in a block of offices that suffered blast damage, 120 ft from the point of impact.

Latchingdon, Essex, 4 miles south of Maldon, at 20.23 hours.

Weybridge, Surrey, on the Thames west of London, at 20.35 hours.

Mayland, Essex, 6 miles south-east of Maldon, at 20.36 hours.

No further data is available to indicate which of the above incidents were caused by the bugs shot down by AA fire but in view of their geographical position there is a strong presumption in favour of Latchingdon and Mayland.

The night of 7/8 October

When eleven Heinkels attacked between 19.55 and 20.30 hours, visibility was good apart from a haze which rose from the sea to little more than 100 ft. Only two missiles aborted at launch but only two terminated their flights according to programme. Seven were shot down, three over the sea.

Stratus cloud at 2,000–3,000 ft over land extended for about 50 miles out to sea.

Flight Lieutenant H. Humphreys and Pilot Officer P. Burton of 68 Squadron from Castle Camps, on anti-diver patrol over the Thames Estuary under Bawdsey control, were vectored on to a missile seen coming from the east at 2,000 ft and 380 mph. Closing to 500 yards they gave it three bursts of fire, following which it disappeared from the radar tube.

A further fly was then seen at 4,000 ft and 280 mph. This time the fighter crew repeated the tactic of the previous night and, getting ahead of it, used their slipstream to upset its automatic control system, sending it tumbling into the sea.

The six that either landed or were shot down over land resulted in the following incidents:

Cheshunt, London, at 20.09 hours. Near Newgate Street off Darnside Hill a doodlebug cratered a field. There were no casualties nor significant damage.

Little Yeldham, Essex, 10 miles north of Braintree, at 20.15 hours. Two cottages were destroyed and sixty other properties, including a school, suffered damage.

Greenstead, Essex, on the eastern outskirts of Colchester, at 20.30 hours. Flight Lieutenant E.L. Williams of 501 Squadron, patrolling between ground beacons, saw this bug coming in at 240 mph and 1,000 ft. He closed to 250 yards and fired three bursts which blew the propulsion unit off the missile, and it went straight down to explode on the ground.

Purfleet, Essex, 14 miles east of central London, at 20.45 hours. This bug fell victim to AA fire.

Sutton at Hone, Kent, east-south-east of Gravesend, at 20.50 hours. A second victory of the night for Flight Lieutenant Williams, this fly fell into a field, but damage was done and five people were injured.

Fawkham Green, Kent, 6 miles south-south-west of Gravesend. This was the second AA score attributed over land. It may, however, have been caught by a barrage balloon cable. It caused both damage and casualties.

The night of 8/9 October

III/KG 3 set a new record this night, with activities divided into three separate attacks, although only a total of fifteen aircraft were employed. Five bombs aborted, and six were shot down by AA over the sea. In the first attack, two missiles fell over land:

Marks Tey, Essex, 4 miles west of Colchester, at 20.00 hours. This doodlebug fell to AA fire. Between 30 and 40 houses were seriously damaged.

Assington Hall, 9 miles north-north-east of Colchester, at 20.04 hours

The *Essex County Standard* told the story of a 3-year-old girl, Linda Rolph, in the Marks Tey incident:

The residents of the village did not hear the approach of the V1 until a terrific explosion wrecked their homes.

The robot, one of a number that came over for the fourth successive night, cut out some distance away unheard until it struck a tree alongside the railway line and exploded.

Little Linda was in bed and although the bomb exploded not far away from the rear of her home it failed to wake her.

Her mother dashed upstairs and although the rafters were down and

debris was all over the bedroom, found Linda fast asleep and unhurt. When aroused she nonchalantly asked, 'What's the matter, Mummy?'

Linda's grandfather, Mr Albert Rolph, was cut about the head and was one of the five persons injured. Another of them, Mr Bert Manning (73) was detained in hospital. The others were Frank Peters (48), Victor Mead (25), and Walter Harvey (72).

The emergency feeding service was soon operating, augmented by the Area Executive Officer's mobile canteen and Assistance Board officers were quickly dealing with claims for various losses, while all day on Monday salvage work went on.

The second attack resulted in the following incidents:

Wangford, Suffolk, 3 miles west-north-west of Southwold, at 00.32 hours. The diver struck elm trees beside the stackyard of Elms Farm. The vivid flash of the explosion was seen by Royal Observer Corps (ROC) observers at Repps, Norfolk, 20 miles away. Severe damage was done to two cottages on the opposite side of the road as well as to the farm. The elm trees were shattered and only survived for a few more years. Two stacks caught fire and a large amount of burning straw was scattered about. The local NFS fire engine was garaged at the Angel Hotel and had only ever been used for Sunday morning practices. On this occasion the motor would not start and the Wangford NFS members were forced to endure the indignity of having to hitch a lift from the Southwold fire tender, which came to help.

Other properties in the village suffered damage; twelve of them were rendered uninhabitable. There were no casualties. The diver was disabled by AA fire before it fell.

Sudbury, Suffolk, at 00.39 hours. The missile fell in the parish of Aveley Hill, 4 miles to the south-east.

Hornsey, London, at 00.52 hours. Two minutes after the alert a diver fell in a garden at 210 Park Road. Casualties were heavy: seventeen people were killed and fifty-four injured, twenty-four of them seriously. Nine two-storeyed terraced houses were wrecked and forty-one others materially damaged. Lesser damaged properties included a cottage hospital.

Saxmundham, Suffolk, at 00.55 hours. The robot was shot down by AA fire and fell 2 miles north at Clay Hills Farm. It exploded against a tree, doing serious damage to the farm and lesser harm to a number of houses, some of which were on the perimeter of the USAAF base at Leiston. The serial number of the missile, 254805, was found on a fragment of wreckage.

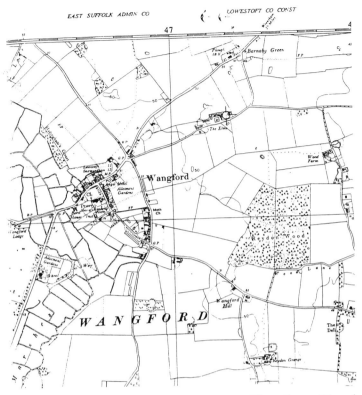

A map showing the location of the V1 impact at Elms Farm, Wangford, Suffolk on 9 October. The location of the Angel Hotel, used by the NFS, is also shown. (Reproduced from the 1958 Ordnance Survey Map with kind permission)

The third attack resulted in only one incident:

> Thwaite St Mary, Suffolk, 13 miles inland from Lowestoft, at 05.12 hours. A bomb impacted in a meadow at Hall Farm, some 300 yards from the Bungay–Thwaite road. There were no casualties but slight damage was done to farm buildings and to the parish church.

The night of 9/10 October
Sunset was at 18.20 hours, and it was to be another night of successive raids, the first between 01.15 and 01.50 hours and the second between 04.30 and 04.50 hours. Intercepted radio messages

from the raiders indicated that 8 *Staffel* was involved in the first and 7 *Staffel* in the second. Four got through, three were abortive and four were shot down by AA, three over the sea.

In the first attack, the bombs fell as follows:

Thurleigh, Bedfordshire, 6 miles north of Bedford, at 00.17 hours.
Billericay, Essex, 24 miles east-north-east of central London, at 00.20 hours. This fly fell to the AA gunners.
Hampstead Heath, London, at 00.39 hours. The diver struck open ground near the junction of East Heath Road and Well Walk, adjacent to an abandoned barrage balloon site. It demolished three empty Nissen huts and blasted some surrounding property. Amongst the wreckage recovered was a steel cable cutter strip from the leading edge of one of the wings.

In the second attack, the following damage was recorded:

Lowestoft, Suffolk, at 04.40 hours. Blast from one of the bombs shot down by AA fire over the sea caused slight damage to eighteen houses and shops ashore.
Potters Bar, London, at 04.43 hours. After an alert at 04.12 hours a bomb fell in a field south of Oakroyd Close, Baker Street.
Hatfield, Hertfordshire, at 04.49 hours. Some damage was done to adjoining property.

The night of 11/12 October
After a break the previous night, III/KG 3 only put up a token show this time. It was provided by 8 and 9 *Staffeln* in an attack which commenced about 20.00 hours and resulted in no missiles getting through – two were abortive and one fell to AA as an airburst over the sea. One shot down over land fell to the guns of Flight Lieutenant E.L. Williams of 501 Squadron at Felsted, Essex at 20.12 hours.

The night of 12/13 October
Two different launching zones were employed on this night for two attacks, the first between 23.30 and 23.50 hours, the second between 04.50 and 05.20 hours.

The launching zone for the first raid was north-east of Great Yarmouth, and this was probably the heavier of the two. The second raid was directed from further south and was the more accurate attack, landing two bombs in the London area. Of seventeen missiles launched, seven were abortive, four evaded the defences and six were shot down, two by AA over the sea.

Incidents reported from the first attack were:

Salcott, Essex, at 23.40 hours. AA fire brought this bomb down in the marshes south-south-west of Colchester.

River Blackwater, 12 miles south-south-west of Colchester, at 23.51 hours. Flight Lieutenant G.R. Birbeck of 501 Squadron in Tempest SD-H caught this diver at 1,000 ft, flying at 340 mph. He fired three bursts from astern, sending it down harmlessly into the river estuary.

Harlington, Bedfordshire, 14 miles south of Bedford, at 23.52 hours.

Stratford St Andrew, Suffolk, 7 miles inland from Aldeburgh, at 23.55 hours. Damaged by AA fire, this doodlebug came near to causing a major explosion. It fell in a wood at Grove Farm only 250 yards from a USAAF bomb dump. Superficial damage was done to seven cottages but there were no casualties. The bomb must have penetrated somewhat before detonating, for there was a massive crater 30 × 15 ft.

Navestock, Essex, 4 miles north-east of Brentwood, at 23.55 hours.

The second attack resulted in the following incidents:

Great Coggeshall, Essex, 13 miles north-east of Chelmsford, at 05.00 hours. Flight Lieutenant R. Bradwell of 501 Squadron in Tempest SD-J on patrol at 4,000 ft saw two divers coming in at 1,500 ft. He chased one of them, travelling at 360 mph, closed from astern and fired four long bursts. The ramjet flame went out and the bomb went down. The diver cratered a field west of Chigwell Road. It caused only minor damage.

Wanstead, London, at 05.08 hours

Friern Barnet, London, at 05.36 hours. One minute after an alert, a missile fell in a garden on the south side of Russell Gardens near its junction with Russell Road. Three semi-detached two-storeyed houses were destroyed, two more were seriously damaged and six others suffered lesser harm. Three people were killed, six seriously injured and a further twenty-nine suffered lesser injuries.

A doodlebug which fell in the sea off Aldeburgh did slight blast damage to seventy-five houses ashore.

The *Essex County Standard* reported on the Great Coggeshall bomb on 20 October: 'More Fly Bombs on villages this week. Early on Friday morning, when flying bombs were released, one of them fell in a field in a tiny hamlet and the blast damaged a cottage. The only casualty was Henry Cullum (67), who was admitted to hospital.'

The night of 13/14 October
On a night of cloud and rain over the North Sea, with gale-force winds blowing from from the north, two attacks came in. The first lasted from 21.10 to 21.40 hours, the second from 03.20 to 03.35 hours. All three *staffeln* took part. The gale resulted in a considerable scattering of missiles over East Anglia, although one did reach the London area. Four were abortive and five were shot down, four by AA over the sea. A total of nine got through the British defences. The first attack resulted in the following incidents:

Great Fransham, Norfolk, 20 miles west of Norwich, at 21.32 hours. At Field House Farm, south of the railway station, a fly detonated, doing damage to the farm and to twelve houses, six of them in Beeston. Fortunately there were no casualties. USAAF personnel took away the remains of the bomb.

Cressingham, Norfolk, 18 miles south-east of Kings Lynn, at 21.45 hours. The fly expended itself on the battle-training area, striking trees south-east of Arms Crossroads. Four civilians were slightly injured, one of them through shock. Serious blast damage was done to houses.

Latimer, Suffolk, 6 miles west of Aldeburgh, at 21.45 hours. The diver fell in the south-west corner of Hyde Wood.

Maulden Wood, Bedfordshire, 6 miles south of Bedford, at 21.49 hours.

Stretton, Rutlandshire, at 21.50 hours. A potentially nasty incident was avoided when a missile fell ½ mile east of Stocken Hall, 8 miles north-west of Stamford. A stock of phosgene poison gas was held at the hall.

Ranson Moor, Isle of Ely, Cambridgeshire, at 21.59 hours. A field was cratered and slight damage caused to surrounding property.

The second attack had the following results:

Worlington, Suffolk, a mile west of Mildenhall, at 03.25 hours
Dagenham, London, at 03.27 hours. A diver hit Hainault golf course.

Beazley End, Essex, 3 miles north of Braintree, at 03.30 hours.

Great Burstead, Essex, on the south side of Billericay, at 03.45 hours. Warrant Officer E. Wojcznski of 501 Squadron claimed this bug. He saw it coming in at 1,000 ft and 300 mph. Closing to 800 yards, he gave it a burst of fire without seeing any results. From 300 yards he fired again, giving it a long burst, during which he closed to 150 yards. The target went down and exploded.

The night of 14/15 October

In a light north-easterly wind with some cloud but otherwise good visibility, there was a heavier raid divided into two attacks, the first between 19.55 and 22.20 hours, the second between 01.35 and 02.05 hours.

No. 7 *Staffel* is known to have been engaged in the first attack, 8 and 9 *Staffeln* in the second. Twenty-two missiles were launched in total, but only three got through. Seven were abortive, seven were shot down over land (two by fighters) and five over the sea (two by fighters).

Flying Officer J.H. Haskell and Pilot Officer J. Bentley, on patrol from 68 Squadron saw a fly on a south-westerly course at 1,500 feet and 340 mph. Closing to 300 yards they fired three bursts and saw 'the light go out'. They saw a second fly coming up behind the first, at 900 ft and 280 mph. This they fired at 'head on' with no result. Changing direction and again closing they fired from a closer range, sending the bomb down into the sea.

The first attack incidents were:

Southwold, Suffolk, at 20.00 hours. Hit by AA fire, a missile detonated over the town, causing injury to a soldier and superficial damage to 230 houses, seventy-nine shops, nine businesses and three churches.

Lowestoft, Suffolk, at 20.14 hours. Damaged by AA gunfire a chuff, as the RAF pilots lightly christened the deadly V1, glided down into the water of the inner harbour. The explosion caused widespread superficial damage to property, particularly in Laundry Lane, fortunately without any casualties. Structural damage was done to buildings occupied by Messrs Brooke Marine Ltd, the Silk Factory, British Petroleum Ltd and the LNER Railway. Some 255 other properties, including two schools, also suffered.

Hopton, Suffolk, 13 miles north-north-west of Stowmarket, at 20.25 hours. Another AA kill glided down into a hedgerow near Back Lane but this time it did not explode. It was heard and reported by Mr Pitcher of Bali Cottage. It was found to have disintegrated but the warhead had not detonated. The tubular mainspar, ramjet and spherical, wire-bound compressed air bottles, were all found intact. Three Royal Engineer bomb disposal officers examined the remains: Major T.J. Deane, the officer commanding No. 10 Bomb Disposal Company, with Captain H. Yard and Lieutenant C.J. Bassett. The warhead had shattered to such an extent that two fuses still in their pockets were separated from the main charge but were still adjacent to it. Clearly they had to be removed. This was done and the pockets with the fuses were laid to one side while the search continued. At 11.05 hours one of the fuses exploded, killing Lieutenant Bassett and injuring the other two officers. The probability is that a clockwork timer attached to the fuse, despite not activating when the weapon disintegrated, started ticking, unobserved, after the relatively gentle movement of being removed from the area of the warhead. The remains of the bomb were taken away by No. 54 MU of the RAF.

The results of the second attack were:

Steeple, Essex, just to the south of the Blackwater estuary, at 01.50 hours. Flying Officer R.C. Deleuze of 501 Squadron, patrolling at 5,000 ft saw the diver below him travelling at 400 mph and held by a searchlight beam. He got into a position astern and in his second attack saw ammunition strikes. Then the bomb lost height and crashed.

Camberwell, London, at 01.52 hours. A direct hit destroyed an air-raid shelter at the rear of houses on the north side of Athenlay Road, near its junction with Fernholme Road. Six brick terraced houses were destroyed and another twenty seriously damaged.

Dovercourt, Essex, at 01.57 hours. This fly fell to AA fire.

Waltham Cross, London, at 02.00 hours. The robot fell opposite 21 Ruthren Avenue amongst semi-detached houses. Three were wrecked and nine seriously damaged.

Tillingham, Essex, 10 miles east of Maldon, again at 02.00 hours. The bug was claimed by AA gunners and fell south of the Blackwater estuary.

Northaw, Hertfordshire, a mile north-east of Potters Bar, at 02.03 hours.

Nayland, Suffolk, 6 miles north of Colchester, at 02.10 hours. The only damage was to turf. Flying Officer R.C. Deleuze scored his second victory of the night here. He saw the missile emerge from the gun belt at about 700 ft and 275 mph. He gave it a three-second burst of fire from an estimated 200 yards and saw strikes before it went down.

The *Essex County Standard* reported on the Steeple incident:

In the early hours of Sunday morning a flying bomb fell in a meadow and caused damage to some houses in a village, four being rendered uninhabitable. Those damaged included a public house. A number of people suffered minor injuries, the most serious being a young girl, Jane Collins, who received cuts to her arms and her head from flying glass.

One of the villagers told our reporter that he did not hear it explode and the first he knew of it was when he woke as the ceiling came down and he was half buried in plaster and glass was strewn over and sticking to the walls. Another resident, Mr Frank Wellesley said that the first thing he heard was a terrific explosion. He was in bed and a shower of glass and plaster fell on him. His two boys were fire watching, which was fortunate for they would have been sleeping where a large part of the bedroom wall fell on the bed.

A neighbouring householder also had a narrow escape when debris fell beside the bed in which he was sleeping.

The robot is believed to have been hit by a plane and pieces of it were found half a mile away.

The night of 15/16 October

Again there were two attacks. The first, launched from a location about 45 miles due east of Orford Ness, lasted from 22.25 to 22.40 hours; the second from roughly 45 miles north-east of Great Yarmouth extended from 04.40 to 05.10 hours. The second was the heavier attack and was more concentrated in direction, being confined to a corridor less than 10 miles wide.

Radio intercepts indicated that aircraft of I/KG 53, which III/KG 3 had become the previous day, took part in the first raid and II/KG 53 in the second. The old III/KG 3 radio call signs continued to be used right up until the first week of November. Of nineteen launches, five got through and five aborted. Nine were shot down by AA, six over the sea. In the first attack the following incidents were recorded:

Luddesdown, Kent, 5 miles south-east of Rochester, at 22.40 hours.

Shopland, Essex, at 22.43 hours. AA gunners on a local site, ½ mile north-west of Barrow Hall, claimed this bug.

Off Beachy Head, Sussex, at 22.43 hours. A stray fly passed over the North Foreland, Battle and the Eastbourne regions of Kent and Sussex before passing out to sea again.

Manea, Cambridgeshire, 6 miles south-east of March, at 22.50 hours.

The following were the results of the second attack:

Benacre, Suffolk, 6 miles south of Lowestoft, at 04.55 hours. AA exploded a fly in mid-air over the coast at Beach Farm. The farmhouse had been requisitioned by the War Office and was occupied by 512 (Mixed) Heavy AA Battery. This and some huts were blasted. Twenty houses in nearby Kessingland were superficially affected. Most of the wreckage of the missile fell into the sea.

Trimley St Mary, Suffolk, 2 miles north-west of Felixstowe, at 04.58 hours. The detonation occurred in Stack Yard Field at Limes Farm, behind the Old Rectory. The church, thirty houses and six other buildings suffered from the blast but there were no casualties. A complete wing of the V1 was torn off and found complete in its grey-green paint.

Chislehurst, London, at 05.05 hours. In the grounds of Holy Trinity Church on the east side of Station Road, a robot detonated on contact with trees. It did much damage to the church, a cinema and modern shops and flats.

Noblesgreen, Southend, Essex, at 05.08 hours. A fly which came in very low struck a ditch at Dandies Farm, 500 yards south of the pumping station.

The night of 16/17 October

Nos. 1 and 3 *Staffeln* are known to have been engaged in a raid by KG 53 lasting from 19.55 to 20.20 hours.

Wing Commander G. Howden and Flying Officer Baker, on patrol in a Mosquito of 68 Squadron were close witnesses to one successful launch. They reported that they made radar contact with a 'bandit' about 50 miles east of Lowestoft. The contact was ahead of them at an estimated 3,000 ft. They chased it at 1,100 ft and then

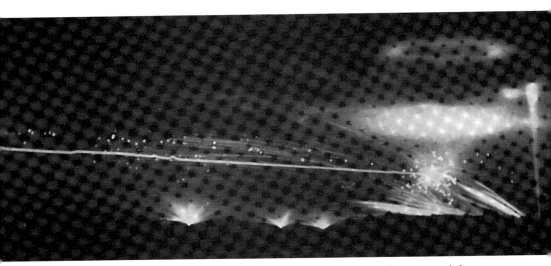

The concentrated firepower of the gun strip accounted for many of the air-launched doodlebugs, some of which were exploded in the air. In this time-exposure photo the pulse jet trail of a V1 is seen coming from the left of the picture. The missile explodes in the air, making a reflected flash and ring of light on the clouds above. A single searchlight beam on the extreme right and gun flashes in the middle ground make an illuminating picture. (Imperial War Museum)

gained height from astern until at 300 yards they obtained a visual sighting under a dark cloud.

Still uncertain of its identity, they closed to about 150 yards, whereupon a huge flash and a flame appeared, gradually diminishing in about five or ten seconds, by which time the flying bomb had dropped several hundred feet and proceeded normally. The He 111 broke upwards to port at the moment of release. To avoid a collision with the bomb, they turned violently to starboard and dived. Contact was not regained.

Of the seven missiles launched, only one evaded the defences. Three aborted and three were shot down, one by AA over the sea. The following incidents were recorded:

Kirby le Soken, Essex, 2 miles inland from Walton le Naze, at 20.18 hours. Shot down by AA into a field 500 yards south of Kirby Road, the robot blasted some houses in the locality.

Ongar, Essex, at 20.30 hours. Flying Officer R.H. Bennett of 501 Squadron, patrolling at 6,500 ft, saw a diver cross the coast at Clacton, coned in searchlight beams. He estimated its height at 1,500 ft and its speed at 450 mph. Diving, he closed on it once clear of the AA gun strip. From 1,000 yards he opened fire with a long burst. Hit, the fly began to climb but exploded at 2,000 ft in an air burst.

Dartford, Kent, also at 20.30 hours.

The night of 17/18 October

This was a particularly good night for the AA gunners, who shot down seven of the eleven bombs launched in a raid lasting from 21.40 to 22.55 hours, five of them over the sea. One was also shot down by a fighter. The remaining three aborted. The three that fell over land were at:

Kirby le Soken, Essex, 2 miles inland from Walton le Naze, at 21.55 hours. Hit by AA fire this doodlebug broke up in the air. The warhead exploded in a grass field a mile east of the village church. The fuselage was found half a mile away from the site of the burst. Some blast damage was done to houses and a farm building. Overhead telephone wires were reported down.

Dengie Marshes, Essex, at 22.05 hours. Good shooting by the AA gunners downed a fly on mud flats near the Bridgwick Outfall.

Grays Thurrock, 2 miles north-west of Tilbury, at 22.13 hours. This fell on waste ground belonging to Thomas Hedley & Co. Although this incident was only 375 ft from a cement works, little harm was done. Warrant Officer E. Wojczynski of 501 Squadron, who was on patrol, saw this doodlebug coming in from the direction of Clacton at 1,000 ft and 370 mph. From astern he gave it a burst without result. Closing to 300 yards he gave it another but then had to break off. He soon saw it explode on the ground.

The night of 18/19 October

The enemy persisted, carrying out two separate attacks of roughly equal strength the following night. The first occurred between 23.10 and 23.35 hours, the second between 04.40 and 05.15 hours. Aircraft of II *Gruppe* are known to have taken part in both attacks.

It was another good night for the AA gunners: they shot down twelve flies, six of them over the sea. In addition, five aborted, leaving two that got through. In the first attack the following incidents were recorded:

At 23.25 hours on Wednesday, 18 October a V1, disabled by AA fire, fell on an Anderson shelter to the rear of 5 Halton Crescent, Ipswich. Five people were killed and twenty-eight injured. Six houses were wrecked and another six seriously damaged in this, the worst of the East Anglian air launched V1 incidents. (David Kindred)

Frinton, Essex, at 23.24 hours. Claimed by the AA gunners, a bug fell on the roadside west-north-west of Frinton Cliffs. It wrecked three homes and badly damaged another. According to the *Essex County Standard* there were a few casualties.

Ipswich, at 23.25 hours. Disabled by AA, another V1 caused the worst flying bomb incident in East Anglia, only 400 yards from Ipswich aerodrome, 2 miles south-west of the town. After an alert at 23.12 hours, an Anderson shelter in the rear of 5 Halton Crescent was struck. Five people were killed and twenty-eight injured in this incident. Six houses were wrecked and another six materially harmed.

Thorrington, Essex, 6 miles south-west of Colchester, at 23.27 hours. Disabled by AA this robot burst in tree tops near Glebe Farm. The missile crossed the coast very low and continued

Damage to Mancroft Towers, Oulton Broad: Shot down by AA fire at 05.11 on Thursday, 19 October, this V1 detonated in trees. Two people were injured. (Bob Collis)

across country until it struck the trees. Twenty houses were seriously damaged and some forty less so.

The *Essex County Standard* said of the Thorrington incident:
> *For the eighth successive night flying bombs came over the east coast on Wednesday night. One bomb which fell in a spinney in a village badly damaged some houses and also a post office and an inn. Many other houses suffered minor damage, together with the parish church and rectory. There were only two minor casualties.*

Weeley, Essex, 10 miles east-south-east of Colchester, at 23.29 hours. Again an AA score and another tree-top burst, this caused blast damage to property and to overhead telephone wires.

Edmonton, London, also at 23.29 hours. This fell in the rear of houses on the east side of Lower Fore Street near its junction with Fairfield Road. Twelve people were killed and twenty-nine seriously injured. Four dwellings were wrecked and two others badly damaged, along with a public house and some lock-up premises.

The *Essex County Standard* reported the 'Heaviest Ever Barrage'.
> *AA guns put up what people in coastal areas described as the heaviest barrage of the war when German flying bombs were launched over the North Sea on Monday night, the sixth night running that bombs have approached the east coast. Observers believed that the defences took their toll of the flying bombs. One bomb had a direct hit and blew up in the air with a great orange coloured flash which lit up the whole sky.*

The second attack resulted in the following incidents:

Oulton Broad, Suffolk, on the western side of Lowestoft, at 05.11 hours. Brought down by AA, a V1 detonated in trees, causing severe blast damage to Mancroft Towers, 200 yards from an LNER railway line. Two people were injured. Mrs Jane Tooke, aged fifty-two, who worked at Mancroft Towers and Mrs Alice Spashett aged fifty-five, a housewife. There was extensive damage also to Woodview, on Prospect Road.

Thurlton, Norfolk, 8 miles west-north-west of Lowestoft, at 05.15 hours. The gunners continued their good work when a diver fell to them on marshland at White House Farm. Twelve houses were blasted and electricity cables severed, but there were no casualties.

Alpheton, Suffolk, 3 miles west of Lavenham, at 05.25 hours.

The night of 19/20 October

Visibility was fair with some haze below and cloud cover above 3,000 ft. There were two separate attacks. The first was launched from a zone approximately 43 miles due east of Lowestoft and had good concentration. The second, launched from about 56 miles east of Southwold, was also tightly concentrated and was well directed. However, only one of the twenty-five bombs evaded the British defences. Six aborted, the AA guns claimed ten (five over the sea) and fighters eight (five over the sea).

Three crews of 68 Squadron were responsible for four of the fighter successes over the sea. Warrant Officer D. Lauchlan and Flight Sergeant Bailey did particularly well, shooting down two. Flight Sergeant Bullus and Flying Officer L.W. Edwards as one crew and Flying Officer G.T. Gibson with Sergeant B.M. Lack each shot down one. From 125 Squadron, Flight Lieutenant R.W. Leggett and Flying Officer E.J. Midlane in Mosquito HK 247 accounted for the remaining one.

Launches were witnessed by two other crews. Flight Lieutenants R.M. Carr and J.S. Saunderson of 25 Squadron saw five launches take place from low level, three of which went straight into the sea. Flying Officers J. Tait and E.P. Latchford saw two, one of which aborted.

The following incidents were recorded in the first attack:

Orford, Suffolk, at 20.15 hours. Amongst trees beside Laurel Farm in the Parish of Chapel St Andrew, ½ mile from Boyton church, this one fell to AA, injuring ten people, three of them seriously. Blast ripped through the farm, and the ramjet unit was found in Chapel Wood, 300 yards south-west of the impact site.
Dengie, Essex, 4 miles south of Bradwell Bay airfield, at 20.25 hours. This too fell to the gunners.

The second attack had the following results:

Ramsey, Essex, 4 miles west-south-west of Harwich, at 04.58 hours. An air burst due to AA fire happened over the marshes south-east of Foulton Hall.
Debden, Essex, 5 miles south of Saffron Walden, at 05.00 hours. Disabled by AA this diver fell in a brook.
Great Bentley, Essex, 7 miles east-south-east of Colchester, also at 05.00 hours. The V1 came down in a field near Frowick Hall without causing significant damage. Flying Officer K.G. Panter

of 501 Squadron saw it coming from the direction of the Naze at 800 ft and 400 mph. He closed to 400 yards, gave it a short burst of fire and saw ammunition strikes. It lost height to 300 ft, where he attacked it again from 200 yards, sending it crashing to the ground.

Fyfield, Essex, 8 miles west of Chelmsford, at 05.06 hours. This bug burst in tree tops near the Fyfield–Great Dunmow road, bringing down telephone wires and doing superficial damage to Pickerell's Farm. Flying Officer Panter saw it flying east to west and gave it a short burst from 300 yards, seeing strikes. It began to climb and at 1,000 ft he gave it a final burst, which sent it crashing.

Stoney Point, Frinton, Essex, at 05.06 hours. Hit by AA fire, this one burst in the air.

Potters Bar, London, at 05.18 hours. There was an impact in a field near the junction of Wagon Road and Barnet Road, South Mimms. Cottages nearby were blasted.

Hatfield, Hertfordshire, at 05.20 hours. In the parish of Brookmans Park a fly fell to Flight Lieutenant R. Bradwell flying Tempest coded SD-J of 501 Squadron.

The night of 20/21 October

Eight launches were made between 04.40 and 05.00 hours, followed by a single launched 1½ hours later. Three were abortive, five were downed by AA (two over the sea) and one got through. The results were as follows:

Great Wakering, Essex, 3 miles north of Shoeburyness, at 04.49 hours. This one was brought down by AA, on farmland.

Barking, Suffolk, 5 miles south of Stowmarket, at 04.50 hours. This landed on the north-west edge of Bonny Wood, on Andrews Farm.

Dovercourt, Essex, near Harwich, at 04.54 hours. The AA gunners claimed this one.

Skippers Island, Essex, 6 miles south-west of Felixstowe, at 06.22 hours. Claimed by AA, this fell in the mud.

Owing to the intensity of the campaign, the serviceability levels of KG 53 aircraft began to fall during this period. Those available for air launch operations on 20 October were stated as:

	Geschwader Stab	I Gruppe	II Gruppe
Aircraft on strength	2	21	40
Aircraft serviceable	0	13	11

Availability was to improve in November.

The night of 21/22 October

The pattern of the previous night was repeated; the main attack developed between 23.00 and 23.15 hours, while a stray missile was shot down only an hour before sunrise. The 'late' arrival was shot down by AA into the sea off Hanford Water, Essex. This secondary launch appears to have been intended to keep the defences active. From radio intercepts 2 and 3 *Staffeln* are known to have taken part. The attack was well directed and three of the missiles reached the London area. One Heinkel of 3 *Staffel* crashed on operations, killing all its crew.

Of the nine missiles aimed at London, only two aborted. The AA claimed one over the sea and fighters three over land. Three made it through the defences. The recorded incidents were:

Rivenhall, Essex, 5 miles north of Maldon, at 23.12 hours. Shot down by Flying Officer J.A.C. Johnson RCAF of 501 Squadron, flying Tempest coded SD-R, this fly landed in a cabbage field north of Colmans farm, which suffered some damage.

Rayleigh, Essex, 3 miles north-west of Southend, at 23.18 hours. Johnson scored a quick second victory here. It fell in the rear of 67–69 High Road, devastating two houses. One detached house and seven semis were also blasted. Gas and water mains were severed and telephone lines brought down.

Cheshunt, London, at 23.30 hours. Eight minutes after the alert a diver slammed into a tree on Hammond Road, causing widespread devastation.

Navestock, Essex, 4 miles north-west of Brentwood, at 23.22 hours. This diver fell to the guns of Flying Officer R.C. Deleuze, flying Tempest SD-Q of 501 Squadron.

Chingford, London, at 23.23 hours. This doodlebug detonated in trees on the southern boundary of Hawksworth House park, causing only minor damage.

Hackney, London, also at 23.23 hours. This struck an Anderson shelter at Prout Road near its junction with Casimin Road.

Two-storeyed brick houses, some with shop premises below, suffered, eight severely, four less so. The Anderson shelter was described as 'buckled'.

As a matter of interest, the bombardment of Belgian cities from V1 launching ramps, first Brussels but later Liège, Charleroi and most heavily, Antwerp, also began on 21 October.

The night of 23/24 October

After a night's pause, there was an increase in the scale of activity on this night, with two separate raids. The first extended from 19.20 to 19.40 hours, the second between 00.40 and 00.50 hours. The first attack centred on a launching zone 44 miles east of Southwold, the second east of Harwich.

Five launches were abortive, six bombs fell victim to AA guns (three over the sea) and two to fighters. Six got through. The results of the first attack were:

Grays, Essex, 2 miles north-west of Tilbury, at 19.40 hours. A direct hit destroyed a single-storey garage on the north side of Orsett Road near its junction with Derby Road. Two people were killed and sixty-nine injured. Destruction was extensive.

Lamarsh, Essex, 5 miles south of Sudbury, at 19.43 hours. AA accounted for this bug, which blew up on Edgars Farm, 300 yards east of the Lion Hotel, doing extensive blast damage.

Ashtead, Surrey, between Epsom and Leatherhead, at 19.50 hours.

Worth, Sussex, 2 miles east of Crawley, also at 19.50 hours.

Woolwich, London, also at 19.50 hours. In Bostall Woods, on London County Council property at the north-east end of Waterdale Road, a robot exploded on impact with oak trees, blasting the trees but having only a minor effect on property.

St Mary Hoo, Kent, between the Medway and the Thames, at 19.55 hours. A diver damaged by AA fire blew itself to pieces.

Incidents resulting from the second attack were:

Dunton, Essex, 4 miles north of Basildon, at 00.53 hours. A diver detonated on striking trees on the north side of the Southend arterial road but caused little harm.

Snape, Suffolk, 5 miles inland from Aldeburgh, at 00.55 hours. Shot down by AA fire, a bug fell on the outbuildings of Rookery Farm, which were devastated. Two men were seriously injured.

Nine heifers were killed. Fragments of the bomb were found perforated by shell splinters.

Bedlam, Sussex, 3 miles east of Petworth, at 01.02 hours. This wide-ranging missile fell 12 miles north of Littlehampton.

Hartlip, Kent, 5 miles east of Chatham, also at 01.02 hours. Two people were killed and one injured when two houses were demolished. Flying Officer D.A. Porter of 501 Squadron, flying Tempest SD-J saw the diver coming from the coast at 1,000 feet and 390 mph. Chasing it, he fired several short bursts before seeing it crash to the ground.

Grays, Essex, at 01.05 hours. Flying Officer R.H. Bennett flying Tempest SD-P saw this fly coming in from the Harwich direction and promptly shot it down.

The I/KG 53 lost one of its Heinkels through a crash. *Obergefreiter* Ealter Hasler, the air gunner, was killed.

The night of 24/25 October

In cloudy, slightly hazy weather, two separate raids were mounted. The first and main attack, lasting from 19.30 to 19.50 hours, came from a zone 46 miles due east of Southwold and was fairly good and tight in direction. The second was brief, lasting from 23.50 to 23.55 hours. Out of thirteen launches, three aborted and two got through. The rest fell victim to AA gunners and fighters. Four were shot down by AA over the sea, and Squadron Leader J.D. Wright and Flying Officer J. McCulloch in Mosquito HK 347 of 68 Squadron shot down two more, also over the sea.

Hits in the first attack were at:

Hartfield, Sussex, 6 miles south-south-west of Tunbridge Wells, at 19.50 hours.

Detling, Kent, 3 miles north-east of Maidstone, at 19.54 hours.

Latchingdon, Essex, 5 miles south of Maldon, at 19.58 hours. The diver fell in an open field at Ullhams Farm, shot down by Flight Lieutenant C.R. Birbeck of 501 Squadron with a few short bursts. He noticed that the ramjet tube was emitting flames from its side before he broke off his attack when the missile passed through low cloud.

Just one incident resulted from the second attack. A diver exploded on impact with trees in a plantation, 1,000 yards south-east of the railway station at Laindon, a mile east of Basildon after AA fire at 00.10 hours.

The night of 25/26 October

With patchy cloud with a base of 500 ft, weather conditions were good for operations on this night. From a launching zone about 42 miles east of Great Yarmouth, a well-directed salvo of missiles came in between 19.15 and 19.40 hours.

Radio intercepts were made on three 1/KG 53 aircraft. Two were preparing to land at Ahlhorn and Varrelsbusch, the third at Hopsten rather than Handorf. Twelve missiles were launched; three aborted and two evaded the defences. The rest were shot down, four over the sea. Squadron Leader M.J. Mansfield and Flight Lieutenant S.A. Janacek of 68 Squadron got one and another fell to an unidentified crew of the same squadron. Two were accounted for by AA.

A crash cost 3/KG 53 one aircrew member, *Feldwebel* Karl Pruksh, a wireless operator. No. 2 *Staffel* lost a whole crew when their Heinkel, piloted by *Oberfeldwebel* Othmar Hammerce, was shot down into the sea by a Mosquito XVII, HK 310, flown by Flying Officers W.A. Beadle and R.A. Pargeter of 125 Squadron.

Incidents were recorded at:

Martlesham, Suffolk, 6 miles east-north-east of Ipswich, at 19.30 hours. The V1 exploded in a small silver birch spinney after it was disabled by AA fire. There were no casualties but two cottages close to the boundary of the airfield suffered.

Boughton, Kent, 3 miles south-east of Faversham, at 19.35 hours.

Downe, Kent, 3 miles south-south-west of Orpington, at 19.39 hours. The missile detonated on impact with trees overhanging Farthing Street, having fallen to Flight Lieutenant R.L.T. Robb of 501 Squadron, flying Tempest SD-Y.

Margaretting, Essex, 4 miles south-west of Chelmsford, at 19.40 hours. Brought down by Flying Officer R.C. Stockburn of 501 Squadron flying SD-U this diver exploded in mid-air and its fragments were found in and about a field 600 ft east of the water tower.

Richmond, London, at 19.55 hours. on the north side of the Golf course at Ham Common a crater 28 × 10 ft was made, but no serious harm resulted.

The night of 28/29 October

A single attack was made between 05.00 and 05.30 hours, after the moon had set. Nine missiles were launched, of which four aborted and four were destroyed, two by AA over the sea. One evaded defences. Incidents were recorded at:

Hollesley, Suffolk, 7 miles north-east of Felixstowe, at 05.10 hours. As a result of AA fire a doodlebug fell in a potato field 500 yards east of Duck Common. Glebe House and twelve other properties were affected by blast but there were no casualties.

Danbury, Essex, 5 miles east of Chelmsford, at 05.18 hours.

Flight Lieutenant E.L. Williams of 501 Squadron saw this bomb approaching his base at Bradwell Bay almost as soon as he was airborne. He climbed to 1,000 ft and the missile passed below him. He closed on it and fired three short bursts from astern, sending it down.

Banstead, London, at 05.45 hours. A direct hit was made on Fincham Lodge, a two-storeyed modern detached house on Copt Hill Lane.

The night of 30/31 October

This was a night of heavy cloud above a base of about 600 ft. There were scattered rain storms.

Two small attacks developed, the first from about 06.30 to 06.40 hours. The second was remarkable because it was the only air-launched daylight attack ever carried out; it despatched missiles from 07.50 to 08.40 hours.

Concern was manifest in defence circles that in bad weather such attacks were possible. Consequently arrangements were made so that, in the event of low cloud and bad visibility by day, two night fighters would be kept at readiness.

There were ten launches in all. Three missiles got through, three aborted and two were shot down over the sea.

Squadron Leader L.W.G. Gill and Flight Lieutenant D.A. Haigh of 125 Squadron under Hopton control in Mosquito XVII HK 325 made AI contact on a 'bandit' at 1½ miles range, flying through broken cloud. They identified it as a Heinkel 111 and gave it a long

Mosquito Nightfighter Mk XVII. This photograph was taken in October 1944 when one of the most important duties the type performed was to hunt the air-launch Heinkels over the North Sea. (RAF Museum)

burst, followed by more. Strikes were seen before the Mosquito overshot and the Heinkel went down to just above sea level. The Mosquito circled and picked up contact with its target again. It had climbed to 600 ft, and at a speed of 180 mph took violent evasive action, but it was unable to escape further bursts of fire from the fighter. It caught alight and crashed into the sea. *Feldwebel* Theodore Warwas, the pilot, and all his crew from 4 *Staffel* of KG 53 perished.

The first attack resulted in a direct hit at 06.50 hours on the Marie Hotel, Coulsdon, London, then used as an old people's private hotel, on the junction of Dale Road and Olden Road. This large brick structure was wrecked and three semi-detached houses were also badly affected. Seventeen people were killed and ten seriously injured.

Ray Denshaw had been invalided out of the RAF the previous day. Woken by the explosion and hearing cries for help he hurried to assist. A policeman said to him, 'Let us see what we can do'. They got seven people out of the wreckage between them before the rescue squads arrived to take over the job.

The results of the second attack were:

Sudbourne, Suffolk, 4 miles south of Aldeburgh, at 07.55 hours. Claimed by AA this bug fell into the marshes.

West Ham, London, at 08.03 hours. A robot fell on the east side of Sullivan Avenue, south of its junction with the Barking byepass. It burst amongst two-storeyed terraced houses, four of which were wrecked and two badly damaged.

Great Wigborough, Essex, 6 miles south of Colchester, at 08.20 hours. Flying Officer A.J. Grottick of 501 Squadron flying Tempest SD-Y shot down this V1 which fell harmlessly on land at Abbots Wick Farm.

Wandsworth, London, at 08.55 hours. The bomb came down in Richmond Park to little effect. It detonated in the area of Roehampton Gate Lodge.

Up to the end of October, the number of sorties flown by squadrons under the control of 12 Group of Fighter Command in over-sea anti-air-launched flying-bomb activities was:

68 Squadron	42 sorties
307 Squadron	92 sorties
125 Squadron	74 sorties
25 Squadron	258 sorties
FIDS Squadron	5 sorties
Total	471

CHAPTER EIGHT

General Pile's Dilemma

On 15 November 1943, as Allied forces in the United Kingdom began to assemble for the invasion of the European mainland, the Allied Expeditionary Air Force Command structure was set up under the command of Air Chief Marshal Sir Trafford Leigh-Mallory, in readiness for the landing planned for the following spring. Part of this structure was set aside for the defence of the British Isles under the title Air Defence of Great Britain (ADGB), under the command of Air Marshal Roderic Hill. This command structure was retained until 15 October 1944, when it was disbanded and the independence of Fighter Command restored.

Amongst the responsibilities laid upon Hill by a directive dated 17 November 1943 was 'to control operationally the activities of Anti-aircraft Command, the Royal Observer Corps, Balloon Command and other elements of air defence formerly controlled by Fighter Command'.

His task was primarily a defensive one and the directive emphasized the need for economy in defence in order to make greater provision for pending European operations.

It is a tribute to both Hill and Lieutenant General Sir Frederick Pile, the chief of Anti-aircraft Command, that the two were able to work together so amicably in what amounted to a chief and subordinate relationship since, whilst both held equivalent service rank, Hill was only appointed in February 1944 as head of Fighter Command, whereas Pile was long established. The difference in seniority and position never seemed to rankle.

Air Marshal Roderic Hill, ably assisted by General Sir Frederic Pile, was the chief architect of the defeat of the flying bomb. His summary of the campaign, published as a supplement to the London Gazette on 19 October 1948, is a masterly piece of historical record. (Imperial War Museum)

The arrival of the first, ramp-launched, flying bombs on the night of 12/13 June 1944, only a week after the D-Day landings was shortly followed by launchings on a much heavier scale. A prompt move was made to deploy all available barrage balloons into a concentrated filter, some 2,000 strong, stretching from Cobham to Limpsfield. This move was accompanied by a redeployment of AA guns into an area south and east of the balloon filter.

The AA gunners were unable to perform to best effect here and a new concept, credited to Air Commodore Ambler, a senior staff officer, was adopted. This involved the redeployment of the AA guns into a belt along the coast from St Margarets Bay to Beachy Head, 15,000 yards deep, extending for one-third of that distance inland and two-thirds over the sea. The obvious advantages of shooting down flying bombs into the sea rather than over populated areas were reinforced by the fact that the guns were now operating with new gun-laying radar sets, the SCR 584 type, which gave better readings when freed from ground contour-interference.

Additionally new variable time (VT) shell fuses were then coming into use which could be employed more effectively and safely over the sea without concern for those shells which missed the target.

The first air-launched missiles to fly in up the Thames Estuary outflanked the gun belt, but the estuary was already defended by Maunsell forts sited well offshore. These steel fortifications were well placed to give warning of the arrival of V1 robots approaching by this route. A 'gun box' was established, incorporating the seven Maunsell forts. This placed guns north and south of the Thames in an area bounded by Clacton and Chelmsford to the north and Wouldham and Whitstable to the south. It incorporated other AA facilities which were already in place and was armed with heavy, mainly 3.7 in guns and also lighter-calibre weapons, mainly 40 mm and 20 mm. The Americans too were able to offer some guns from the total of twenty AA batteries of 90 mm guns they contributed to the overall diver defence.

As we have seen, to provide the necessary guns for the belt and box there was an almost total withdrawal of AA units from a line drawn across the country from north of the Humber to west of the Solent. The risk to the areas thus denuded of AA guns was considered acceptable in view of the limited range of the V1 as then understood, and the fact that the conventional German bomber force was largely spent in the west. Yet more guns were found for the south-east by selectively thinning out other defences.

The location of the gun box and the gun strip to counter the air-launched flying bombs aimed at London from the east. (Author's map)

On 11 September the intelligence section of ADGB issued a warning that the possibility of further attacks on Britain by flying bombs launched from aircraft could not be dismissed, although the ground-launching sites had been overrun. Activity might be expected in the 12 Group area of Fighter Command.

This warning was issued against a background of planned reductions in AA Command already agreed by the Chiefs of Staff on 6 September. These involved the disbandment of 93 heavy batteries (744 guns) and 31 light batteries (372 guns). Fifteen searchlight batteries (360 searchlights) were also to be axed. The intention was, in the light of the reduced air threat, to provide more men for the army on the continent. The objections of the Ministry of Home Security were overridden.

The War Office, however, was unable to absorb all these men immediately and it was agreed to let them stay active in the AA structure until they were required.

The gun belt proved so successful that it seemed a good idea to extend it to other parts of the coast which later needed protection from the incursion of air-launched flying bombs. The barrage balloon screen was extended up to the Thames at Gravesend but no further. After ramp-launching ceased at the end of August, General Pile considered that, since balloon cables tended to interfere with gun-laying radar, any extension might hinder the defence of London against orthodox air attacks.

In July the movement of the AA guns into a gun belt on the south coast proved so successful that it set the precedent for anti-diver defence in the box and strip. (Imperial War Museum)

When III/KG 3 regrouped in Germany and recommenced launching on 16 September they systematically outflanked the gun box and the missiles came inland more to the north-east, over the Essex and Suffolk coasts. Hill and Pile made the decision to extend the gun defences northwards along the coast by adding a 'gun strip' from the left of the gun box, where it joined the coast at Clacton, progressively up to Great Yarmouth. The necessary guns for this were obtained largely by thinning out the belt on the south coast, which was anyway now largely redundant.

Operational orders to deploy the guns into the strip north of Clacton were issued between 16 and 19 September. The strip was to be 5,000 yards deep. The speed and enthusiasm shown during the move into the belt in July was not apparent this time, and it took some three weeks to complete the move. The occupation of the strip was done in stages, the first being between Clacton and Harwich. By the middle of October 498 heavy and numerous light guns were deployed in the box and strip. The existing local defences of Harwich and Lowestoft were integrated into the strip.

Amongst the most active AA units was 142 (Mixed) Regiment, which had both male and female soldiers. It deployed 261 Battery at Great Baddow, 2 miles south-east of Chelmsford, 488 Battery at Bradwell, 16 miles east of Chelmsford, and 433 and 477 Batteries at Stanford le Hope on the north bank of the Thames, 6 miles north-north-east of Tilbury.

One AA regiment posted in was 138, whose 424 and 438 Batteries arrived at Aldeburgh on 29 September. Its 419 Battery arrived in the Lambert's Grove area and 437 Battery in Thorpness, both on 26 September.

General Pile wrote:

> In many ways it was a pity that so much public stress was laid, at the end of the first phase of the [V1] battle, on the greatness of the triumph and on the finality of the victory … which had entailed a fearful amount of both physical and mental strain, which, coming as it did at the end of five years of war, had told upon us more than we realized. The unwelcome reopening of the battle disclosed an unexpected weakness in the defences. It was not so much a material as a spiritual weakness and it arose entirely out of a sense of anti-climax.
>
> The first symptoms of this weakness were a general lassitude on the part of the staff, a great disinclination to start the whole weary business over again.

At the beginning of September the diver gun box contained 136 static 3.7 in guns, 210 guns of 40 mm (only 74 of which belonged to AA Command) and some 20 mm guns manned by the navy and RAF Regiment. There was also one Z rocket battery.

Between 16 and 19 September both light and heavy AA guns were ordered into the strip, but just as they were starting to move, the news came that the enemy was launching attacks to cross the coast well to the north of Harwich.

Again to quote General Pile:

It looked at that moment as if the Luftwaffe *had got us properly on the run. As fast as we moved northward, so might the Hun each time anticipate us and from our point of view there was a limit to this northward trend. The manpower cuts had left us [AA command] a mere shadow of our former selves . . . The only thing we could do was to extend our attenuated forces as far as we could and live in pious hope that there was some kind of limit to the area over which the enemy could*

General Pile's close working relationship with his nominal chief, Air Marshal Roderic Hill, contributed significantly to success against the air-launched flying-bomb attacks. (Imperial War Museum)

deliver his attack, or that he would prefer to batter away at London in preference to northern England.

It was realized that the diver strip, as the gun strip was sometimes called, was going to lie across the track of Allied bombers flying to and from the Continent and that extreme care would be needed not to shoot down our own aircraft. General Pile stated:

Full scale deployment into the diver strip began on the morning of 22 September with the intention that the guns should be in action in four days, the same time limit that had been met in the July redeployment. Many new problems arose, however, and the vigorous management of July was this time lacking.

When on 2 October, the deployment had still not been completed General Pile sent out a teleprint:

The deployment into the diver strip has been deplorable and reflects great discredit on every one of us . . . Everywhere there is some reason for shame . . . Everyone is trying to put the blame on someone else. Let us instead get on with the job and so put matters right.

Not until 13 October, eighteen days later than had been intended, was the redeployment of some 300 static guns completed, in a strip stretching from Clacton up to Southwold. The gun positions had in some cases to be modified later to allow firing at a much lower angle than normal, owing to the low height at which most flying bombs were found to be coming in. The same applied to the gun-laying radar equipment. Nevertheless by the end of October, the box-strip defences amounted to 542 heavy and 503 light, mostly 40 mm, guns. Some 2,000 miles of communication cable had been laid.

By that time, positive results were being achieved in terms of the percentage of incoming bombs destroyed, matching those previously obtained on the south coast. The manpower cuts agreed on 6 September, however, put this success at risk. It drained off many of the younger men and with them went their skills and expertise. It is much to the credit of AA command that the standard of training was somehow kept up despite all the reshuffling, so much so that by the end of November 82 per cent of all targets coming within range of the guns were hit.

The problems of the searchlight units initially matched those of the gunners. There had originally been eleven batteries of searchlights deployed at the normal 6,000 yard spacing layout, capable of engaging any target flying at 2,000 ft with between three and seven beams. At the lower heights at which many flying bombs came in, however, engagement was much more difficult. This could only be remedied by reinforcement. Another seven searchlight batteries were brought in to increase the concentration to intervals of 3,000 yards between searchlights in a zone 16 miles deep.

As winter closed in the living conditions on the gun and searchlight site caused increasing concern, and the press and some members of parliament caused rather a stir. A visit by the Speaker of the House of Commons to see for himself and the rapid construction of huts to replace the tents eased the situation.

A study paper was drawn up 'to determine in what areas heavy AA guns with SCR 584 Gun Control Radar and No. 10 Predictors [to aim the guns based on the radar information] would have to be deployed to protect the Midlands and the West Riding from flying bomb attack and what equipment and manpower would be required'.

Drawing on London's experience it was presumed that the enemy would launch their missiles from 30–60 miles off the east coast at the limit of the CHL radar coverage. The paper postulated that from the southern limit at Spalding, an extended gun strip, to be called the 'gun fringe' should join up with the existing Tees (estuary) gun defended area (GDA), and various gun spacing options were evaluated. Finally, on 21 October it was agreed that 408 guns in 45 batteries would be made available to deploy on the coast from Spalding up to the River Tees.

On the proposed fringe there were CHL radar stations at Cresswell, Danby Beacon, Saxton, Bampton, Easington, Skendlesby and West Beckam, and GCI facilities at Seaton Snook and at Dimlington on Humberside. One was also planned for Goldsborough between Whitby and Staithes on the North Yorkshire coast, should this prove to be necessary.

On 2 November, 5 AA Group, then in the south-east, was ordered to carry out a detailed reconnaissance for deployment into that part of the coastal fringe stretching from Skegness to Whitby. While this was being done by officers down to battery commander level, the group commander, Major General W.W. Green, ordered the guns and their platforms to be disposed so that the sites chosen could be occupied rapidly in the section between Mablethorpe and Hornsea. This was considered to be the enemy's most likely entry point in the event of an attack upon the North Midlands industrial area.

Planning for the move included anticipatory arrangements for the billeting of troops, and even involved the setting up of some gun platforms in advance. This greatly facilitated the movement into the fringe when it finally came about. Officers and NCOs selected for the move were all either experienced in, or given specialist training in, the techniques of shooting down flying bombs.

On 19 November General Pile's plan for the extension into the gun fringe was completed and submitted to the General Staff for approval, with a request for authority to commence the redeployment at his discretion. It provided for the use of fifty-nine batteries, including those already in the Humber GDA. The proposed AA Brigade HQ were to be at Loftus, Whitby, Scarborough, Bridlington, North Coates, Mablethorpe, Skegness and Boston.

By 9 November, Fighter Command HQ at Bentley Priory was showing signs of some agitation at the increasing scale of air-launching activity, anticipating thirty-six launches per night in the near future and ninety-six by the spring of 1945. They also noticed 'signs of German concentration on pathfinder techniques to improve the accuracy of air launching' and asked for the conversion of twenty-seven light AA batteries to produce twenty-one heavy ones.

Bomber Command, on the other hand, which had a great concentration of airfields in use in Lincolnshire and Yorkshire, wanted to limit the creation of the gun fringe as much as possible to avoid what they saw as a hazard to their own aircraft. The General Staff, faced with conflicting pressure, delayed its decision, and despite repeated requests from AA Command, permission to move into the fringe was not forthcoming until events forced the issue.

In the early hours of Sunday, 24 December the feared attack on the north finally came. General Pile was then given immediate authority to move sixty heavy AA guns into the fringe, followed four days later by four searchlight sections. This was a more powerful force than mere numbers would suggest because of the new, sophisticated gun-laying equipment and ammunition which accompanied the guns.

General Pile declared that using this new equipment the average number of heavy AA rounds fired for each V1 destroyed was 156.

Air Chief Marshal Sir Roderic Hill (as he had by then become) referred to the problem posed by the passage of friendly aircraft over the gun strip and by implication the gun fringe, in his published summary of UK air defence against the V weapons, which appeared as a supplement to the *London Gazette* on 20 October 1948.

The changed direction of attack [air launching from the east] brought new problems. For various reasons, of which the chief were the imminent

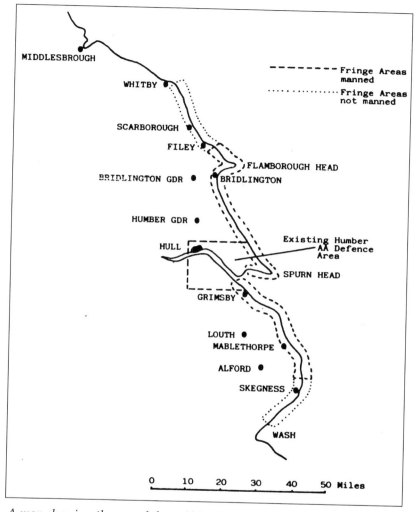

MIDDLESBROUGH

WHITBY

SCARBOROUGH

FILEY

— — — — — — — Fringe Areas
manned

· · · · · · · · · · · · · · Fringe Areas
not manned

FLAMBOROUGH HEAD

BRIDLINGTON GDR · · BRIDLINGTON

HUMBER GDR ·

Existing Humber
AA Defence
Area

HULL

SPURN HEAD

GRIMSBY

LOUTH ·
MABLETHORPE ·

ALFORD ·

SKEGNESS

WASH

0   10   20   30   40   50 Miles

*A map showing the gun-defence 'fringe' planned for the protection of
the Midlands and northern industrial areas from air-launched flying
bombs.* (Author's map)

*character of the attacks and the geographical position of our own bomber
airfields, I could not give the gunners the same freedom that they had
enjoyed in the south-east during the summer. Although I was able to
establish the principle that flying over the box or strip below 6,000 feet
should be prohibited in normal circumstances during the hours of*

darkness, I was forced to defer to the needs of Bomber Command to the extent of permitting their aircraft to fly over the strip, although not the box, at any height they pleased provided they gave prior warning to my headquarters. The concession entailed a corresponding restriction of gunfire. I also had to reserve the right to restrict gunfire at any other time in order to safeguard friendly aircraft which for one reason or another were unable to avoid flying low over the strip to reach their bases.

His account also details the experience of co-operation between fighters and searchlights:

The Tempests, which had been outstandingly successful in countering the main attack in the summer, now operated with the aid of searchlights in a belt extending from Saffron Walden to Sudbury in the north and Southend to Brightlingsea in the south. At first these searchlights were deployed at intervals of 3,000 yards. Experience showed that so thick a spacing tended to dazzle the pilots and we altered the interval to the normal 6,000 yards.

Experience also taught them that night-intruder missions by Mosquitos to bases used by the carrier Heinkels achieved little, so they were curtailed from 7 October. It was found that if Mosquitos were scrambled as soon as air-launch activity was detected, they could often reach the enemy bases before the Heinkels returned.

Bombing operations against these airfields were requested but so marked was the lack of enthusiasm for this in Bomber Command that Hill wrote of his concern to the Chief of Air Staff, but with little result. By the middle of October the Chiefs of Staff evidently took the view that the British home defences were sufficient to contain the air-launched V1 offensive and that Allied bombing efforts were better directed elsewhere.

Jointly with the Telecommunications Research Establishment (later the Royal Radar Establishment) the Fighter Interception Development Squadron (FIDS) developed an anti-air-launch tool which in later years was to become a vital part of modern air warfare, the Airborne Early Warning Communications System (AWACS). The low-flying tactics of the carrier Heinkels suggested that existing air to surface vessel (ASV) radar used to locate enemy vessels, particularly surfaced submarines, or even their conning towers, might be adapted to locate a low-flying Heinkel. A Wellington bomber was therefore fitted with an ASV set and a homing beacon onto which the SCR 729 tracking set of an accompanying FIDS Mosquito was tuned. This enabled the two aircraft to keep in constant contact, the fighter ½ mile behind the

Wellington. The ASV radar operator in the Wellington could then control the pilot of the fighter by radio to intercept any suspicious radar plots picked up.

The first trial was scheduled for 2 January 1945 off the Dutch coast, the Wellington making an elongated orbit over the anticipated Heinkel approach route. Control of the ASV radar was in the hands of a scientist, E.J. Smith. The Wellington worked up and down a 57 mile stretch of the coast selected but no enemy appeared. Three nights later at a second trial the ASV became unserviceable.

Next, on 13/14 January the Wellington was accompanied by an FIDS Beaufighter in place of the Mosquito, and this time a number of apparent targets were located. One, which was flying slowly westwards, was selected by the ASV radar operator. It showed a firm blip on the radar screen and looked promising. The Beaufighter was directed onto it and closed at an overtaking speed of about 30 mph. The fighter crew identified the target using night binoculars, but it turned out to be another Wellington. The interception had drawn the Beaufighter away from the real Heinkels, but at least the system had been proved to work. There were no other opportunities, for this was to be the last air-launched flying bomb raid.

The fitting out of HMS *Caicos* with radar to patrol as a seaborne radar control interception station in the area over which launchings were expected to take place was completed just too late and was never tested in action. The ship was nevertheless anchored some 20 miles off Harwich, ready for operations.

On a practical level, one of the problems associated with night-fighter interception of flying bombs was judging the range, even with the help of searchlights. It was straightforward enough to see the light of the pulsejet flame; the problem arose in estimating the distance to the bright light. Then the spectro-scientist Sir Thomas Merton devised a simple yet effective gunsight to meet the need.

CHAPTER NINE

November – The Busiest Month

A full moon at the beginning of November passed towards the end of the first week and it soon became apparent that the scale of effort KG 53 was able to apply had almost doubled. November was to be the busiest month of the campaign.

The night of 4/5 November

Darkness came under a cold, overcast sky with a 34 mph wind blowing at 2,000 ft from the east-north-east.

New radio call signs specific to KG 53 were brought into use for the first time, but of course the Germans were aware that their radio traffic was subject to monitoring by the British and all transmissions were kept to a minimum. They were usually made only when aircraft were returning to base.

Only one attack developed, starting at 19.06 hours and ending at 19.42 hours. Twenty-four Heinkels were engaged but only twenty-three reached the launch zone, for one fell to a Beaufighter, V8565 coded ZQ-F, which was on detachment to Coltishall from the Fighter Interception Development Squadron at Ford in Sussex, for the purpose of testing the benefit of its lower stalling speed over the Mosquito in engaging the slow flying Heinkels. The experiment was a success but the Mosquito crews were resentful and circumspection was thought necessary.

Squadron Leader Jeremy Howard-Williams, who with his observer Flying Officer F.J. MacRae crewed the Beaufighter, reported that under Hopton GCI control he was directed towards a 'bandit' and got an AI fix at 1½ miles range. When he was in visual

A manufacturer's photograph of the Bristol Beaufighter. This type had a lower stalling speed than the Mosquito and was proved by the fighter Interception Development Squadron to be suitable for engagement of the carrier Heinkels, but the matter was not followed through. (BAe Systems plc)

range he identified it as a Heinkel 111 with a flying bomb under its starboard wing. One long burst started a big fire in the Heinkel, which dived straight into the sea, complete with the bomb. Williams then chased another Heinkel which he and MacRae saw launch a fly, but this time the enemy got away.

The Heinkel they shot down was a serious loss to KG 53, for it was piloted by a very experienced *staffelkapitan, Hauptman* Heinz Zollner, commander of 4 *Staffel* and a Knights Cross holder. His observer *Oberfeldwebel* Karl Christmann was also a Knights Cross holder. The other crew members were *Feldwebel* Erich Schnider, *Oberfeldwebel* Fritz Marhoun and *Feldwebel* Leonhard Dollmeer.

KG 53 lost two other Heinkels in the operation, evidently due to accident, one from 4 the other from 5 *Staffel*.

The amount of AA ammunition fired by the British that night is on record as 1,364 rounds of 3.7 in, 193 of 40 mm and 278 of 0.5 in machine gun.

Of the twenty-three launches, eleven were abortive, six were shot down over the sea and five over land, and just one evaded the defences. Recorded incidents were:

Debden, Essex, at 19.14 hours. Shot down by AA, this bomb fell into trees behind Seabridge Cottages, ½ mile east of Stratton Hall, 3 miles south of Saffron Walden. One person was killed and four injured when the cottages were badly blasted.

Breckles, Norfolk, at 19.23 hours. Nine miles north-east of Thetford, Breckles Hall and Breckles Church suffered blast damage when a diver exploded in a field at Grange Farm.

Brentwood, Essex, at 19.30 hours. A 'score' to AA fell in a stubble field at Bushwood Farm on the outskirts of the town, causing superficial damage.

Ongar, Essex, at 19.33 hours. Flight Lieutenant E.L. Williams, flying Tempest SD-L of 501 Squadron shot this bug down into a potato field just west of Flanns Cottages, Berners Roding. No serious damage was caused – except to the bomb.

Radwinter, Essex, at 19.42 hours. Flight Lieutenant D.A. Porter, in SD-K of 501 Squadron, despatched a fly into a ploughed field 4 miles east of Saffron Walden. It fell only 40 yards from a railway line.

Southminster, Essex, at 19.51 hours. AA hit a fly which fell in marshes ½ mile south-west of Turncole Farm on the north bank of the Crouch Estuary. Damage was done to the farm buildings. Enemy propaganda leaflets were found at the scene, bearing the headline, 'V1 – those last few shots' in mockery of Duncan Sandys's assurances to the British public. More will be said about leaflets in a later chapter.

The night of 5/6 November
Poor weather conditions prevailed, with dense cloud above 2,300 ft and a 31 mph wind from the west-north-west at 2,000 ft. It seems that the *Luftwaffe* weather forecasters may have miscalculated this, for an unusually high proportion of the missiles strayed to the south of London. A single raid starting before 19.20 hours finished at 20.30 hours.

A Mosquito crewed by Flight Sergeant L.W. Mead and Flight Sergeant E. Eastwood claimed the destruction of one Heinkel, and another was missing as a result of an accident. The Germans posted the following aircrew as missing:

From 6 *Staffel*: *Leutnant* Heinz Redde, pilot; *Obergefreiter* Herbert Jung, navigator; *Feldwebel* Peter Weinand, wireless operator; *Unteroffizier* Erich Bogan, flight engineer; and *Obergefreiter* Richard Parzinski, airgunner.

From 7 *Staffel*: *Unteroffizier* Walter Schulz, pilot; *Obergefreiter* Gunter Kudszus, navigator; *Obergefreiter* Werner Gasner, wireless operator; *Unteroffizier* Helmut Reichmann, flight engineer; and *Unteroffizier* Karl Kuchler, airgunner.

Owing to an apparent miscalculation in navigation, at least one Heinkel of II/KG 53 strayed over the Kent coast before releasing its missile. It must have been blessed with extraordinary luck not to have been shot down in the process. It was the first enemy-piloted plane to cross the British coast since 22/23 October.

Of twenty-seven launches, fifteen were abortive, three were shot down by AA (two over the sea), and nine managed to get through. Reported incidents were:

Winchelsea, Sussex, at 19.33 hours. This bomb strayed well to the south-west and fell only 6 miles short of Hastings and close to the south coast.

Shoreham, Sussex, at 19.37 hours. Further west along the south coast, this missile fell between Brighton and Worthing.

1.8 miles south-west of Wisborough Green, Sussex, at 19.41 hours.

Frant, Sussex, at 19.45 hours. Extensive damage was done to Frant Place, 3 miles south of Tunbridge Wells. A girl was injured here and propaganda leaflets entitled 'The Other Side No. 1' were found.

Crawley, Sussex, at 20.02 hours. A diver fell to the east of the town.

1½ miles north-east of Steyning, Sussex, 5 miles east of Worthing, at 20.04 hours.

After overflying parts of Kent and Sussex at 20.11 hours, a missile went on to explode in the Channel.

Telescombe, Sussex, 6 miles east of Brighton, at 20.14 hours.

Aldeburgh, Suffolk, at 20.21 hours. AA fire brought a doodlebug down onto an AA gun site. This was a remarkable incident in several ways. The missile failed to explode when it struck No.

3 gun on site S7 of 438 Battery of 138 HAA Regiment. One gunner was severely burned and three were slightly burned by petrol from the bomb's ruptured fuel tank, ignited by residual flame from the pulse jet. The warhead detached itself from the body of the missile and fell onto the gun-laying radar equipment. The site was also an ROC observer post, from which two shaken observers reported to their HQ at Colchester that 'diver 286 had passed within ten feet of their post, with motor still running and that it had set light to the gunners' tents'. The observers pluckily sought permission to evacuate the post as the warhead had not exploded and there was AA ammunition stacked nearby. It was subsequently discovered that the warhead had split into pieces on impact.

Kennington, Kent, 2 miles north-east of Ashford, at 20.44 hours.

The night of 6/7 November
The increased level of activity was maintained. Another concentrated attack was launched between 20.10 and 20.40 hours. It was seen by Flight Lieutenant S. Woodward and his crew in a Liberator of 223 Squadron operating in 100 Group of Bomber Command. They saw at least twelve flying bombs approach the coast east of Woodbridge, five or six of which were shot down by the coastal AA gunners. One missile passed only an estimated 300 ft astern of Woodward's aircraft.

It was a good night for AA, who shot down seventeen of the twenty-seven missiles launched, twelve over the sea. Nine aborted, leaving just one to get through the defensive barrier. Those that came down fell at:

Westleton, Suffolk, 8 miles north of Aldeburgh, at 20.18 hours. Shot down by AA onto moorland ½ mile east of Walkbarn Farm, the missile caused no serious damage.

Tendring, Essex, 9 miles east of Colchester, at 20.22 hours. This fly too fell to AA. It damaged Fishers Farm and other surrounding property.

Kelsale, Suffolk, between Saxmundham and Yoxford, at 20.31 hours. No casualties were reported but eight houses were damaged. The badly damaged tube of the pulse jet and the main spar of this bug were later displayed at the Norfolk and Suffolk Aviation Museum at Flixton.

Foulness Island, Essex, 5 miles north of Shoeburyness, at 20.35 hours. AA brought the missile down into a ploughed field. There was some damage to buildings at Eastwick Farm.

Great Oakley, Essex, 6 miles south-west of Harwich, at 20.46 hours. This kill fell to AA fire north-north-west of Maltings Farm, doing some blast damage to what was described as old property.

Bapchild, Kent, 2 miles east of Sittingbourne. This was the bomb that evaded the defences.

The night of 8/9 November
After a pause of one night, KG 53 was out in increased strength, making a single raid, which started at 20.10 hours and finished at 21.00 hours.

A map produced by the Essex County Standard newspaper showing the fall of flying bombs on and off the Essex and Suffolk coast. The crosses indicate falls due to AA fire and the dots those which ran their course. Those doodlebugs which fell to fighter action are excluded from the map. (Essex County Standard)

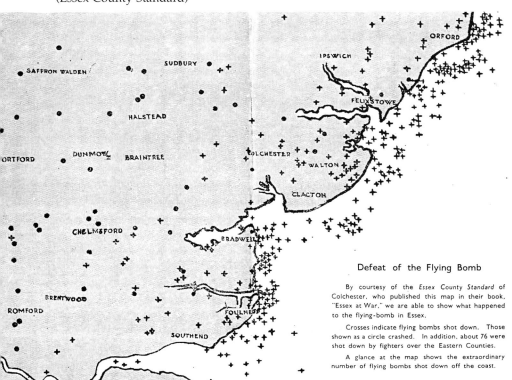

Defeat of the Flying Bomb

By courtesy of the *Essex County Standard* of Colchester, who published this map in their book, "Essex at War," we are able to show what happened to the flying-bomb in Essex.

Crosses indicate flying bombs shot down. Those shown as a circle crashed. In addition, about 76 were shot down by fighters over the Eastern Counties.

A glance at the map shows the extraordinary number of flying bombs shot down off the coast.

The weather was reported to be half clouded-over at between 1,000 and 3,000 ft, with otherwise good visibility and a wind of 38 mph from the north-north-west. It was not ideal for this operation and the *Luftwaffe* weather forecasters appear to have underestimated the wind strength, judging by the number of missiles falling in Kent.

Aircraft of 3, 5 and 6 *Staffeln* are known to have taken part in the raid, launching thirty-two missiles. Thirteen of these aborted and seven evaded the defences. AA accounted for eight more (five over the sea) and fighters for four (two over the sea). Reported incidents were:

Stockbury, Kent, 6 miles SE of Chatham, at 20.21 hours.

Detling, Kent, 2 miles NE of Maidstone, at 20.25 hours.

Northbourne, Kent, 2 miles inland from Deal, at 20.25 hours.

Rochester, Kent, at 20.45 hours. A direct hit was made on a modern terraced house on the west side of Grafton Avenue, near its junction with Gerrards Avenue. Eight people were killed, seventeen seriously injured and over thirty suffered lesser injuries when six terraced houses were wrecked and another thirty-two materially damaged. Some 575 houses suffered minor damage.

Newington, Folkestone, Kent, at 20.48 hours. The missile impacted to the west.

Leadon Roding, Essex, 9 miles NW of Chelmsford, at 20.49 hours. Blast Damage was done to Leadon Roding Hall. Flight Lieutenant R Bradwell, on patrol in SD-J of 501 Squadron got this bug which he saw approaching from the east at 800 ft. He closed and fired a burst from astern. The missile lost speed but kept on course. Three more bursts caused the 'flame to go out'.

Swanscombe, Kent, between Gravesend and Dartford, at 20.49 hours.

Four Elms, Kent, 8 miles west of Tonbridge, at 21.02 hours.

Meopham, Kent, 6 miles west of Chatham, at 21.03 hours. This bomb fell victim to AA fire.

Ivy Hatch, Kent, 5 miles east of Sevenoaks, at 21.04 hours.

South Stifford, Essex, on the northern edge of Grays, at 21.07 hours. By great misfortune this bomb fell in the front garden of 7 Palmerston Road, a mile west of Grays railway station, amongst two-storeyed terraced property, wrecking four houses, severely damaging five and doing minor damage to over 500. One person was killed, twenty-three seriously injured and fifteen lightly hurt.

Flight Lieutenant D.A. Porter, flying Tempest SD-K of 501 Squadron saw it approach from out of the gun box and moved astern of it, closing to 600 yards. He fired but the missile continued on course. Firing again he saw strikes and then it appeared to be on fire. Another burst sent it crashing down.
Frant, Sussex, 3 miles south of Tunbridge Wells, at 21.14 hours.

The night of 9/10 November
A 41 mph wind blew from the north-north-west and there was a half-cloud covering with a base at 1,000 ft. Visibility was otherwise good. All serviceable KG 53 aircraft were mustered for a double attack. The first and heaviest commenced at 18.45 hours and concluded at 19.15 hours. The second started at 21.35 hours and ended at 22.15 hours.

Radio transmissions were intercepted coming from Heinkels of 2, 3, 4 and 6 *Staffeln*. One Heinkel is reported to have briefly made landfall.

The Operational Record Book of 25 Squadron at Castle Camps has an entry for the night of 9 November, written in the debonair jargon of the time:

> *Tonight the Hun boobed badly and the Squadron let him have it smartly between the eyes. P/O D.J. Carter with P/O W.J. Hutchings, in their devil-may-care manner, shot down a flying bomb and later in the evening F/Lt. J. Lomas and F/Lt. N.B. Fleet, throwing discretion to the winds, shot down a Heinkel 111.*

Eleven of the twenty-nine launches were abortive and four evaded the defences. Ten bombs were shot down over the sea (one by a fighter) and the rest over land. The first attack resulted in the following hits:

Walthamstow, London, at 19.08 hours. A direct hit was made on Reliance Foundry on the east side of Oatlands Rise, near its junction with St Andrew's Road. The foundry was a brick building with steel trusses and sheet asbestos roof cladding, together with a shed-type trimming shop. It was totally destroyed, as was the nearby one-storey brick Salvation Army hall. Nine houses were also substantially damaged.

Lullington, East Sussex, 5 miles north-west of Eastbourne, at 19.10 hours.

Throwley, Kent, 4 miles south of Faversham, at 19.12 hours.

East Grinstead, Sussex, at 19.20 hours. A fly with its engine still running exploded on striking trees, doing blast damage to

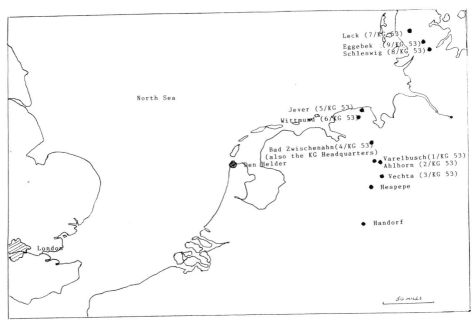

A map showing the location of airfields used by Kampfgeschwader 53 *and the radio beacon at Den Helder.* (Author's map)

twenty houses and causing a casualty. Propaganda leaflets headed 'The Other Side No. 1' were found at the impact site.

Dengie, Essex, 3 miles south of Bradwell Bay, at 19.28 hours. Shot down by AA the fly cratered a ploughed field without much effect.

The results of the second attack were:

Ramsey, Essex, 2 miles west of Harwich, at 22.03 hours. AA fire exploded a doodlebug in mid-air. Most of the debris fell in a turnip field south-east of Newhall Farm.

Brentwood, Essex, at 22.05 hours. Three people were killed and eight seriously injured when there was a direct hit on 8 Mount Crescent, east of its junction with Warley Mount. Semi-detached houses took the worst of the blast: three of them were wrecked and five seriously damaged. The missile was on a course for London until it was intercepted by Flight Lieutenant Bradwell in Tempest SD-J.

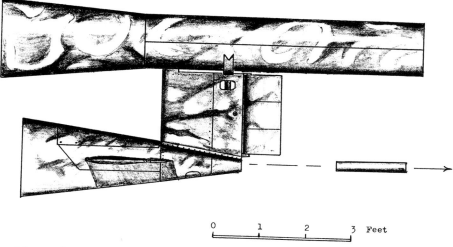

0   1   2   3 Feet

The cardboard tube of propaganda leaflets ejected from the tail cone of a flying bomb. This was done by a small explosive charge, and a second charge scattered the leaflets. (Frank Leyland)

Minster, Kent, 4 miles inland from the North Foreland, at 22.26 hours. This missile fell to the AA gunners.

The night of 10/11 November
Half-cloud over the North Sea had a base at 800 ft. In the middle of the sea there was a patchy cloud belt down to sea level in places. It was a night of occasional rain with a wind speed of 23 mph from the south-south-west at 2,000 ft. These were good conditions for an attack and every serviceable KG 53 Heinkel was put up to make this the heaviest raid of the whole air-launched flying-bomb campaign.

The assault was divided into two separate attacks. The first and weightiest commenced about two hours after sunset, at 19.22 hours, and finished at 19.48 hours. The second was a briefer affair, lasting from 01.20 to 01.30 hours. As in previous attacks there were separate launching zones.

It cost the enemy three carrier Heinkels.

At 19.10 hours, A1+AB W.Nr 162080 of *Gruppe Stab* I/KG 53 fell to Flight Lieutenant G.F. Simcock and Flying Officer M.E. Heijne in Mosquito HK 263 coded VA-M of 125 Squadron. They only claimed a 'probable'.

Then in the second attack, at 01.30 hours, A1+NM W.Nr 161924 of 4 *Staffel* was shot down by Flight Lieutenant D.H. Greaves and Flying Officer F. M. Robbins in Mosquito MT 492 of 25 Squadron under Bawdsey GCI. They obtained a sighting of it at a height of 200 ft and opened fire with a long burst from dead astern, seeing strikes which were followed by a sheet of flame about the starboard engine and wing root. Wreckage was left burning on the sea when the Mosquito resumed its patrol.

At 01.55 hours, A1+BM W.Nr 700862, also of 4 *Staffel*, was downed by Flight Sergeant A.R. Brooking and Pilot Officer R.B. Finn, flying Mosquito HK 348 of 68 Squadron. They saw four divers released and got an AI contact flying at 700 ft with a speed of 180 mph. This led to a visual sighting at 1,200 ft. Flying through patchy cloud they closed to 600 ft, where the Mosquito opened fire and the crew saw hits. Pieces flew off the starboard wing root and fuselage, and a glow of burning was visible inside the fuselage. The Mosquito crew broke off the combat to avoid flying wreckage and a few seconds later they saw the Heinkel burning on the sea.

Over the whole night forty-eight flying bombs were launched, of which fifteen aborted. The AA gunners performed well above average by shooting down twenty-five of the thirty-three missiles that approached the coast, of which twenty-one were shot down over the sea. Only four evaded the defences but two of these fell in the London Civil Defence Region. One flying bomb was shot down over the sea by Pilot Officer D.J. Carter and Pilot Officer W.J. Hutchings of 25 Squadron, flying in Mosquito MT 474.

The nearest abortive bomb in the raid is reported to have fallen 12½ miles from the coast. Tempest fighters of 501 Squadron in their usual role as long stops of the defences did well to shoot down three of the eleven robots which crossed the coast.

The results of the first attack were:

Wymondham, Norfolk, 5 miles west-south-west of Norwich, at 19.45 hours. One person was injured when a fly caused minor damage to Browick Hall Farm and to six houses. The electricity supply to a nearby USAAF base was cut off.

Writtle, Essex, 1½ miles west of Chelmsford, at 19.47 hours. Impact with trees in a wood south-east of Little Moor Hall caused minor damage. Flight Lieutenant H. Burton, in Tempest SD-Z, saw this missile held in searchlights at Walton before chasing it to destruction.

Ufford, Suffolk, 4 miles east of Woodbridge, at 19.50 hours. No casualties were reported but St Audrey's Mental Hospital and

Grove Farm were amongst the premises that suffered superficial blast damage.

Shotley, Suffolk, 4 miles east of Felixstowe, at 19.58 hours. AA fire accounted for a bug which fell between the rivers Orwell and Stour, on the verge of Shotley High Road and also close to HMS *Ganges* naval establishment's recreation ground. Superficial damage was caused to houses.

Ash, Kent, 5 miles south-south-east of Gravesend, at 21.01 hours. One person was killed when a house was demolished and others damaged.

Incidents resulting from the second attack were:

Orford, Suffolk, at 01.30 hours. A doodlebug despatched by AA fire fell in Watling Wood ½ mile north of Sudbourne Hall, then a War Department property. The hall suffered slight damage.

Clacton, Essex, at 01.42 hours. There was an impact in a grass field south-west of Barkham's Farm.

Hunsdon, Hertfordshire, 3 miles north-north-east of Harlow, at 01.49 hours. This stray fly was shot down by Flying Officer J. Maday in Tempest SD-V of 501 Squadron.

Dagenham, London, 10 miles from central London, at 01.50 hours. On the south side of Osbourne Square four houses built of brick and breeze blocks were seriously damaged, as were two Anderson shelters.

Great Warley, Essex, 3 miles south-west of Brentwood, at 01.52 hours. This was the second victory of the night for Flight Lieutenant Burton. Damage was done to Codham Hall when the missile fell in a field 200 yards to the east of it.

Beckenham, London, 8 miles from the centre, at 01.53 hours. The robot exploded on impact with trees in the rear of 1 and 3 Copers Cope Road, three-storeyed detached brick houses. They were badly damaged and there was extensive other blast damage which included sheds at the Southern Railway goods yard at Beckenham Junction Station.

The night of 13/14 November

This was a cloudy night with occasional rain and a 45 mph wind blowing from the north-west. After a short pause following the major effort of the 10th/11th, perhaps for serviceability reasons, KG 53 resumed operations with a single attack which started at 17.55 hours, only forty-five minutes after sunset, and finished about 18.20 hours.

The strong crosswind may have contributed to the high number of abortive bombs – eleven out of twenty-one. Intercepted signals indicated that 1, 3, 4 and 6 *Staffeln* were engaged. Only two missiles got through, the rest were shot down by AA (five over the sea). Incidents reported were:

> Hockley, Essex, 5 miles north-west of Southend, at 18.22 hours. Falling to AA fire into a field just north of Hockley Hall, this diver did extensive damage to cottage property.
>
> Eastchurch, Kent, near the Swale Estuary, at 18.24 hours. Downed by AA onto the Isle of Sheppey this one exploded in the marshes.
>
> South of Thames Haven, Essex, at 18.25 hours. This diver fell to AA, impacting in mid-Thames.
>
> Sible Headingham, Essex, 5 miles north of Halstead, at 18.26 hours. This one exploded in a plantation north of the church but did no serious damage.
>
> Cooling, Kent, 1½ miles north of Cliffe, at 18.26 hours. This one fell on marshes.

The night of 14/15 November

The raiders were back in strength, this time launching a triple attack which coincided with the firing of six V2 rockets at London so that the city was under intermittent fire substantially throughout the night.

Misleadingly high British estimates taken from radar returns, showing seventy-one aircraft involved, led to unfounded speculation that some KG 53 aircraft might be making more than one sortie per night. Nevertheless, with only two *gruppen* yet operational, KG 53 were hard pressed to provide the serviceable machines it did operate.

Three separate launching zones were adopted, the first about 40 miles north-east of Lowestoft, the second around 55 miles east of Bawdsey and the third to the south of the other two. The attack took place in conditions of low cloud over the North Sea with rain, sleet and snow. At 2,000 ft a wind of 30 mph blew from the southwest. The first raid lasted from 18.40 to 19.20 hours, the second from 23.55 to 00.40 hours and the third from 05.25 to 05.45 hours. Thirty-seven missiles were launched, of which thirteen aborted and thirteen were shot down (seven over the sea). Of the eleven that got through the defences, eight reached London.

It was an unsatisfactory night for the nightfighters, indeed a tragic one. There were no claims of enemy aircraft destroyed but two of the fighters were lost, both of them to British AA fire. Mosquito MV 526 of 25 Squadron piloted by Wing Commander W.J. Mitchell, with Flight Lieutenant D.L. Cox as his observer was hit off Southwold whilst returning home short of fuel, and crashed in a moat at Uphill Farm, Garboldisham, 11 miles east of Thetford in Norfolk. The crew baled out successfully but Mitchell sprained his ankle.

The second Mosquito was HK 289 coded WM-K of 68 Squadron, crewed by two US naval airmen, Lieutenant Joseph Black and Lieutenant Thomas Aiken, who were both killed. They were attached to the Squadron for familiarization with RAF techniques. They took off from Castle Camps airfield at 18.05 hours for an anti-diver patrol over the North Sea. It appears that they made contact with a Heinkel which they saw release a doodlebug before they could close with it. They decided to chase the doodlebug and in their enthusiasm followed it into the AA gun strip, where they were shot down. Ironically the missile escaped the gunfire to fall near Berkhamsted in Hertfordshire. The Mosquito crashed in a field at Decoy Farm, Flixton, 18 miles west-north-west of Lowestoft. Both airmen were posthumously awarded the US Air Medal and the Purple Heart. A memorial stone to them was erected in a lane near the crash site by Lord Somerlayton, the landowner.

Misfortune dogged the Germans too. Heinkel H-22 coded A1+KP of 6 *Staffel* abandoned its mission due to trimming trouble and crashed while attempting an emergency landing, killing two of its crew. No. 4 *Staffel* lost another in a crash landing which killed a crew member, *Unteroffizier* Georg Fiebig.

In the first attack bombs fell as follows:

Middleton, Suffolk, 3 miles south-east of Dunwich, at 18.45 hours. Winged by AA, this bomb did some damage to a farm and four houses.

Falkenham, Suffolk, 9 miles east-south-east of Ipswich, at 18.58 hours. Another AA victim, this one exploded on a hedgerow embankment south of Lower Farm, damaging the farmhouse and some wooden outbuildings.

Glemham, Suffolk, 5 miles south-east of Framlingham, at 19.00 hours. AA knocked this one down into trees at Glemham Park. Blast damage extended to the hall, the church, the rectory and four cottages.

Cuxton, Kent, 3 miles west of Chatham, at 19.08 hours.

Martlesham, Suffolk, 7 miles east of Ipswich, at 19.14 hours. Believed to have been damaged by AA fire, this V1 exploded just south-west of the Martlesham–Newbourne road. Superficial damage was done to some thirty semi-detached houses.

Friern Barnet, London, at 19.15 hours. After an alert at 19.07 hours the missile fell at the rear of flats on the east side of Sydney

Road, near its junction with Hampden Road. Extensive damage was done to flats, and an Anderson shelter was demolished. Two people were killed here and ten seriously injured whilst twenty suffered lesser injuries.

South-west of Berkhamsted, Hertfordshire, at 19.27 hours. This was the V1 that Lieutenants Black and Aiken chased.

These were the results of the second attack:

Rayleigh, Essex, 6 miles north-west of Southend, at 00.12 hours. A fly which came in very low, having been damaged by AA fire, hit 121 Rayleigh Road, leaving no crater. Detached, semi-detached and terraced properties suffered extensive damage.

Felsted, Essex, 5 miles west of Braintree, at 00.15 hours. Rutland Farm and nearby cottages were damaged when a fly exploded in a field.

Croydon, London, at 00.15 hours. A two-storeyed detached house was demolished on the east side of Castlemain Avenue, south of its junction with Ballasten Road. Other properties were badly damaged and a small fire started by petrol from cans stored in a domestic garage. Propaganda leaflets headed 'The Other Side' were found nearby.

Pembury, Kent, 3 miles east of Tunbridge Wells, at 00.20 hours

St Pancras, London, at 00.30 hours. Eighteen people were killed and twenty injured when a pair of semi-detached homes were demolished and adjacent property damaged on Grafton Road near its junction with Warren Road. To the rear of these houses a glass factory, Chas Pugh (Glass) Ltd, and a garage, General Roadways Ltd, were severely damaged.

Little Bentley, Essex, 5 miles east-north-east of Colchester, at 00.31 hours. The missile fell to AA. Minimal damage was caused.

Sutton, London, at 00.58 hours. Eleven people were killed and eighteen injured when a V1 exploded on hitting trees on Henley Avenue near its junction with Windsor Avenue. Two-storeyed brick semi-detached and terraced houses were destroyed or damaged.

The third attack had the following results:

Surbiton, London, at 05.50 hours. One house was destroyed and another badly damaged when a V1 exploded in a front garden on the west side of Ashcoombe Avenue, near its junction with Woodlands Road. A gas main was fractured and set on fire.

Bethnal Green, London, again at 05.50 hours. A robot exploded on the west side of Treadway Street. Brick terraced houses, some of which had previously been blitz-damaged were affected. Seven were destroyed and a 4 in gas main was broken and set alight.

Fyfield, Essex, 8 miles west of Chelmsford, at 05.53 hours. A bungalow was seriously damaged when a ploughed field nearby was cratered.

The night of 17/18 November

Just one raid was made on this night, starting about 18.50 hours and finishing at 19.30 hours. Continuing bad weather, whilst it provided cover, may have contributed to a high rate of abortive launches. Out of 23 launches made, 13 aborted (nearly 57 per cent). Mosquitos of 456 Squadron operating out of Ford airfield, Sussex, were assigned for the first time to anti-air-launch patrols off the Dutch coast and flew some five sorties, although they were unable to down any of the Heinkels. Five bombs were shot down by AA fire over the sea, two over land and three got through. The following incidents resulted from the raid:

Orsett, Essex, 5 miles north of Tilbury docks, at 19.21 hours. One person was killed and sixteen injured when widespread damage was done by a missile which impacted in a meadow at Great Holland Farm.

Hadleigh, Essex, 4 miles west of Southend, at 19.23 hours. AA fire brought down a V1 onto brick semi-detached houses on the north side of Church Road near its junction with Woodfield Road. Eleven people were killed and others injured when four of the houses were destroyed.

Rayleigh, Essex, 3 miles north-west of Southend, at 19.23 hours. Hit by AA fire, this one burst amongst trees in Rawreth Hall Wood, some 300 yards from a sewage works.

Fristling, Essex, 4 miles south-west of Chelmsford. A diver that fell in a ploughed field near Fristling Hall did no serious damage.

Buntingford, Hertfordshire, 9 miles east-south-east of Letchworth.

The night of 19/20 November

The cloud base was down to about 600 ft but visibility was good under the cloud base. The night's operations began a period of reduced activities. For the rest of November the number of carrier aircraft fell to about half the average for the previous couple of weeks. On 20 November KG 53 reported thirty-eight machines as serviceable.

From 456 Squadron, an Australian crew of Flying Officer D.W. Arnold and Flying Officer J.B. Stickley flew an anti-diver patrol under Trimley ground control and at 20.15 hours saw a V1 launched. They obtained an AI contact and then a visual sighting of a Heinkel at 700 ft. It began weaving and went down to 400 ft. They followed and fired three bursts. The Heinkel returned fire, slightly damaging the starboard propeller of the fighter, but then caught alight and climbed to 1,200 ft before crashing into the Zuider Zee – now the Ijsselmeer. *Luftwaffe* records show it to have been Heinkel 111 H-16, coded A1+NN, of 5 *Staffel*, piloted by *Feldwebel* Rudolf Ripper, who perished with his crew. Years later their bodies were recovered from the wreckage and interred at Leeuwarden cemetery in Holland.

Of the thirteen launchings, only three aborted, but only one evaded the British defences. The rest fell victim to AA fire, seven falling over the sea. Recorded incidents were as follows:

Carlton Colville, Suffolk, 4 miles south-west of Lowestoft, at 19.57 hours. Shot down by AA, this robot demolished two cottages and damaged farm buildings, five houses and a modern bungalow. Over 100 premises received minor damage. Agnes Grimble, a housewife aged sixty-two and Edith Ribbans, a housekeeper aged fifty-four, were both killed. Seventeen people were injured in the incident. Propaganda leaflets headed 'The Aftermath No. 6' were found scattered near the site.

Copford, Essex, 4 miles south-west of Colchester, at 20.15 hours. Hit by AA fire a diver blew up in a field east of Seven Sisters Green. Slight damage was done to houses about ½ mile away.

Brickenden, Hertfordshire, 5 miles south-east of Welwyn, at 20.36 hours. There were no casualties but twenty-three houses suffered slight damage when a bomb exploded in a field east of a sewage farm. Leaflets headed 'The Other Side' were found near the site.

The night of 22/23 November

A raid was carried out between about 00.45 and 01.05 hours. There was a sea fog up to 1,000 ft and thick cloud at about 6,000 ft.

Warrant Officer J.L. Mulholland and his observer, Flying Officer J.D. James, in Mosquito HK 317 of 456 Squadron, chased a Heinkel which they saw launch a V1, carried, they asserted, under its port wing. They did not break off the pursuit until they were 20 miles inside Dutch airspace. The weather finally frustrated their effort.

The crater and damage done by the air-launched doodlebug which fell at Carlton Colville at 19.57 on Sunday 19 November. The missile was shot down by AA fire, demolishing two cottages as well as damaging farm buildings, five houses and a modern bungalow. Two people were killed and seventeen injured. (The late Mr Jeff Gorrod)

Heinkel 111 H-20, works no. 700638, coded A1+KH, of I/KG 53 lost two of its crew members killed when it crashed near Osterode.

From 68 Squadron Flight Lieutenants Peebles and Grinndal were scrambled for anti-diver patrol but crashed shortly after taking off. Their Mosquito broke up on hitting the ground near Horstead Hall and both airmen were killed.

Of ten launched this night, three aborted and six were shot down, three by AA over the sea.

The results of this raid were:

Great Burstead, Essex, 3 miles north of Basildon, at 00.55 hours. A field at Frith Farm was cratered and there was some minor blast damage.

Wherstead, Suffolk, 5 miles south of Ipswich, between the rivers Stour and Orwell, also at 00.55 hours. This missile exploded after it was brought down by AA fire into trees on the northern edge of Cutlers Wood. The nearby church and fifteen houses took some blast damage. There were no casualties.

Sudbourne, Suffolk, 2 miles north of Orford, at 01.12 hours. Shot down by AA, this doodlebug fell on open ground 90 ft east of Captain's Wood.

Harlow, Essex, 1½ miles south of the town at 01.18 hours. Flight Lieutenant H. Burton in Tempest SD-Z of 501 Squadron shot this missile down onto open ground east of Hubbards Hall, where it caused only slight damage.

The night of 23/24 November

Elements of both *gruppen* took part in a raid which was launched between 05.30 and 05.50 hours. Five bombers aborted.

Warrant Officer J.L. Mulhall and Flying Officer J.D. Jones, in their Mosquito HK 317 of 456 Squadron, failed to return from patrol. They were posted as missing after descending to 50 ft in an attempt to engage a Heinkel. Their loss may be attributed either to having hit the waves or to return fire from the enemy. Jones, from Ystalyfern, was just twenty-two.

The defences again showed their mettle. Ten out of sixteen missiles were shot down, six by AA over the sea. Only one evaded the combined efforts of the AA guns and the fighters. The following incidents were recorded:

Colchester, Essex, at 05.43 hours. A mile from the town centre, a brick two-storeyed cottage was badly damaged and the blast affected surrounding property, including overhead wiring. The fly was claimed by the AA gunners.

Dovercourt, Harwich, Essex, at 05.50 hours. Another AA claim this bug fell near High House but burst on open ground, doing only minor damage. Propaganda leaflets found near the site were gathered in by the police.

Kirby Cross, Essex, 1½ miles west of Frinton, also at 05.50 hours. This fly cratered a ploughed field north of the railway station. Some blast damage was done.

Springfield, Essex, a mile north-east of Chelmsford, at 06.06 hours. Flight Lieutenant Burton scored when he exploded this fly in mid-air.

Boxford, Essex, 10 miles north of Chelmsford.

The night of 24/25 November

With the approach of a full moon, this night's operations were to be the last for November. Ten days were to elapse before they resumed. There was a single raid, with launches lasting from about 04.45 to 05.10 hours.

Luftwaffe records note the loss on operations of a I/KG 53 Heinkel, works number 160304, coded A1+BH. The body of one crew member was subsequently washed up at Bergen (Holland); the others remained on the missing in action list. Flying Officers F.S. Stevens and W.A.H. Kellett, an Australian crew of 456 Squadron in Mosquito HK 290 coded RX-J, shot this aircraft down 10 miles west of Texel. The burning wreckage was seen to bounce over the surface, leaving a 'sea of flames'.

Ten launches were made, of which only one escaped the attentions of the British defences. Six aborted and the rest were accounted for by AA fire, two over the sea. The results of the raid were as follows:

Great Bentley, Essex, 7 miles inland from the Naze, at 04.22 hours. This diver fell to AA fire on grassland south-east of Admirals Farm, doing minor blast damage to a number of cottages. Leaflets were found nearby headed, 'A Splendid Decision'.

Hampstead, London, at 05.04 hours. An explosion at the rear of 61 King Henry's Road wrecked numbers 59, 61 and 63, all of them early nineteenth-century three-storeyed houses. Extensive blast damage was done to surrounding property. Twelve people were killed and twenty-nine seriously injured.

CHAPTER TEN

December – Past the Worst

Air-launching activity, which had ceased for more than a week, resumed on the night of 4/5 December. It was the work of III/KG 53 which had been identified by British intelligence authorities as under training up to that time.

According to the British evaluation the nominal strength of the three *gruppen* which now together formed KG 53 was about 100 carrier aircraft, enough to provide a serviceable strength of between sixty and seventy machines, each of which could carry one flying bomb on each mission. The threat appeared to have increased markedly.

There was no shortage of flying bombs, for the ramp launches against continental targets proceeded apace. From 25 November 1944 to 15 January 1945, 1,654 bombs were ramp fired, and other evidence pointed to ample stocks being available. Nor was there any reason to believe that crew losses were not being replaced.

In fact nothing like the calculated potential appeared. Despite the fact that three *gruppen* were now operational, the scale of effort for the remainder of the air-launched campaign was never to match that of early November.

A straw in the wind was contained in the British Weekly Intelligence Report of 22 November: 'It is considered that the low scale of effort during the last week by units engaged in flying bomb launching is not wholly attributable to bad flying weather or bad airfield conditions. Growing fuel difficulties are thought to have contributed, which are likely to continue.'

A model of a Heinkel III H-16 with a V1 attached for air launching. (Author's photograph)

The night of 4/5 December
A single attack between 19.00 and 19.30 hours came from a northerly launching zone due east of Lowestoft. The south-westerly course of the missiles, which reached the coast in the Felixstowe area, exposed them to coastal AA for a prolonged period, and this was reflected in the number shot down by the gunners. Of eleven launched, seven were downed over the sea. Three aborted. The sole evader fell at some time between 19.10 and 19.40 hours at East Malling, 3 miles west of Maidstone, Kent.

The night of 5/6 December
The previous night's attempt was repeated in greater strength between 20.10 and 20.30 hours. However, of fifteen bombs launched

Secrets of the New-Style Doodle-Bug Revealed

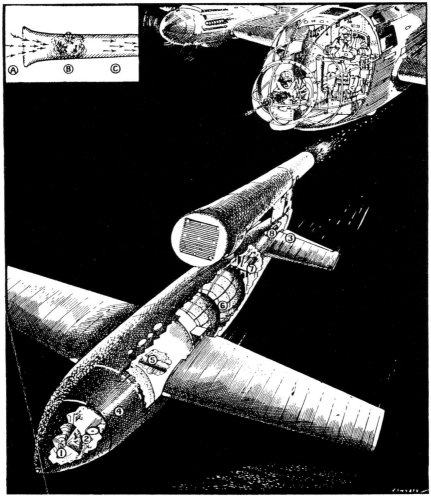

PLANE-LAUNCHED FLYING BOMBS used by the enemy in renewed attacks against this country were described by Mr Duncan Sandys, Parliamentary Secretary to the Ministry of Supply and Chairman of the Flying Bomb Counter-Measures Committee, on October 31, 1944, as being *under* the launching planes (semi-obsolete Heinkel 111s), contrary to previous principles governing composite aircraft and as shown in page 405. They were probably released in the same way as torpedoes or rockets carried by R.A.F. Typhoons, though the risk to the air crews, as well as the take-off difficulties, were considerable. Carrier-planes were said to fly only a few feet above the sea, rarely venturing nearer than 50 miles to our coast. In this sectional drawing, pilot and observer in the Perspex "nose" of the Heinkel are seen as the bomb is launched. Points of interest are (1) small propeller driven by the bomb's flight, and (2) the electric revolution-counter. When the propeller has registered a set number of revolutions, the elevators (3) are automatically moved into "diving" position, thus urging the bomb to earth. Other bomb-parts are (4) warhead, containing 2,000 lb. of explosives; (5) tubular main spar passing through the fuel tank, which has a capacity of 330 gallons; (6) wire-bound compressed-air bottles which inject petrol into the engine; (7) automatic pilot, which keeps the bomb on a set course; and (8) rudder- and elevator-operating mechanism. The inset shows the working of the large impulse-duct engine. (A) Air stream through the grille to be compressed (B) simultaneously with the injection of petrol. The mixture is then fired by a spark, thus closing the valves. The white-hot gases are then emitted (C), propelling the bomb on its flight.

PAGE 469 *Specially drawn for* THE WAR ILLUSTRATED *by Haworth*

A representation of the air launching of a flying bomb from under the wing root of a Heinkel, as shown to the British public in December.
(The War Illustrated)

only one got through. Eight aborted and three were shot down over the sea (two by AA). The rest fell to AA and fighter fire over land. The raid resulted in the following incidents:

Takeley, Essex, 5 miles west of Great Dunmow, at 20.25 hours. Shot down by AA fire, this fly exploded in tree tops at Colchester Hall farm, destroying a barn and four wooden farm buildings.

Manuden, Essex, 3 miles north of Bishops Stortford, also at 20.25 hours. Flight Lieutenant H. Burton, in SD-N of 501 Squadron, shot this bug down into a wheat field, where it burst with little effect. Burton reported that he sighted it flying at 900 ft and at 350 mph, caught up with it and gave it two medium bursts so that 'the light went out' and it crashed.

Chignall St James, Essex, 2 miles north-east of Chelmsford, at 20.30 hours. Squadron Leader A. Parker-Rees, in Tempest SD-P, shot this diver down onto grassland near the Bishops Stortford–Chelmsford road. He reported that it was flying at 400 mph and 1,000 ft. He gave it three bursts of two seconds each, saw strikes and the 'light go out', followed by an explosion. Some damage was done to Chignall Hall just north of the impact.

Walthamstow, London, at 20.32 hours. After an alert at 20.24 hours a V1 detonated in trees at Oak Hill, a large house in its own grounds situated at the eastern end of Holly Crescent. Extensive blast damage resulted.

The night of 7/8 December
Launching took place between about 18.30 and 18.55 hours from a zone centred 50 miles east of Orford Ness. The projected course of the missiles tracked indicated a well-directed attack, but still only one evaded the British defences. A further eight aborted and nine were shot down over the sea by AA. Of three shot down over land, two were accounted for by AA. The following incidents resulted:

East Hornon, Essex, 4 miles south-east of Brentwood, at 18.50 hours. Flight Lieutenant D.A. Porter in Tempest SD-K shot this one down ½ mile south-east of East Hornon Hall. Two haystacks were burned and overhead telephone wires were brought down; otherwise only slight damage was done.

Foulness Island, Essex, at 18.51 hours. AA accounted for a V1 which exploded in a field at Nazewick Farm on the north-western part of the island. It caused little damage.

Chelmsford, Essex, at 18.55 hours. North-east of the town centre a bug fell in the back garden of a house on Springfield Road. While substantial damage was done to the surrounding property, the explosive force seems to have been largely expended on blowing a large crater 31 × 6 ft.

North of West Mersea, Essex, on Mersea Island, at 18.59 hours. Another AA score, this missile fell in a grass field off Prince Albert Road. Wooden bungalows with tiled roofs were damaged and an overhead electricity cable brought down.

Hans Hoehler, a wireless operator in KG 53, flew his first operational mission this night. His plane took off from 3 *Staffel*'s Vechta airfield shortly after 18.00 hours under a low cloud base. Passing over Emmen, Steenwijk and the Zuider Zee, they reached Den Helder, where the *zahlwerk* mechanism was activated. The total outward flight took about half an hour. Immediately after the launch of their V1 the pilot banked away with such vigour that Hans 'almost brought up his lunch'. He flew again in attacks on London on 10, 12 and 18 December and Manchester on 24 December, but never reconciled himself to sitting in an illuminated carrier plane whilst the missile got away.

The night of 10/11 December
In this attack directional accuracy was poor and the robots were scattered from Bedfordshire to Kent.

No. 1 *Staffel* lost a Heinkel piloted by *Unteroffizier* Gunter Lis and the whole crew were listed as missing in action. It seems that the aircraft disappeared over the North Sea. Fifteen launches were made, of which seven aborted and three got through. The rest were accounted for by AA fire, two of them over the sea. The results were:

Walton on the Naze, Essex, at 18.50 hours. AA exploded a diver in mid-air over the sea but this was so close to the shore that some damage was caused to buildings on the coast.

Chelmondiston, Essex, 4 miles south of Ipswich, again at 18.50 hours. Hit by AA fire, this V1 fell on Myrtle Cottage only 50 ft from the parish church. The cottage was destroyed and the church heavily damaged. Nineteen houses suffered serious damage and some sixty were also affected. Mr Rands of Myrtle

Cottage was killed and twenty people were injured. This tragedy in the life of a rural community was in later years recorded in *Fifty Years On*, a small book by Elizabeth Crawford for the benefit of the restored church.

Levington, Suffolk, on the opposite bank of the River Orwell to Chelmondiston, at 18.53 hours. Damaged by AA fire this missile burst amongst trees in a hedgerow at Red House Farm, doing some damage to the roof, windows and outbuildings of the farm.

Tottenham, London, at 19.03 hours. After an alert at 18.34 hours a direct hit was made on 112 Fairfax Road. Seven terraced two-storeyed houses were destroyed and another eight seriously damaged. Some sheds at the rear of the property were set on fire. This incident cost the lives of thirteen people and another eighty-eight were injured, twenty-four of them seriously.

Kirby le Soken, Essex, 3 miles inland from Walton.

Great Barford, Bedfordshire, 5 miles east-north-east of Bedford. The bug fell at Northfields Farm, setting fire to straw and cutting electricity cables.

The night of 11/12 December
This attack lasted from 22.30 to 23.10 hours. Elements of II and III *Gruppen* took part. Half the fourteen launches were abortive, but four got through. AA fire accounted for one shot down over the sea and two over land. The following incidents were recorded:

Hopton, Norfolk, 6 miles south of Yarmouth, at 22.40 hours. The weapon made landfall and impacted at Whitehouse Farm. It disintegrated without exploding, scattering its components over an area 100 yards long. Captain Yard and twelve bomb-disposal men of the Royal Engineers attended the site where a search revealed scattered explosives and other evidence that the warhead had broken up. The explosives were collected and detonated in the hole made by the force of the impact. Following Lieutenant Bassett's death on 15 October the bomb-disposal team was very wary of V1 fuses and it was thought that unexploded fuses might lie with other wreckage in the impact hole. The jet propulsion unit, rudder, elevators and two spherical compressed air bottles were all recovered.

Monkton Barn, Essex, 8 miles north-east of Southend, at 23.06 hours. Hit by AA fire, this robot fell in the middle of the River Roach, causing no damage.

Burnham on Crouch, Essex, at 23.06 hours. Derelict Tyle Barn
Farm on Wallasea Island suffered damage from a bug shot
down by AA fire.

Hanningfield, Essex, 5 miles south-south-east of Chelmsford, at
23.13 hours. This fly fell in a field north-west of Pattons Farm
without significant damage.

Beddington, London, at 23.14 hours. The missile struck the north
side of Westcote Avenue, damaging property and fracturing a
4 in gas main and electricity cables.

Rainham, Essex, 2 miles east of Dagenham, at 23.15 hours. A
bomb burst on impact with trees just south of Berwick Pond
Farm, north-east of Rainham railway station. Severe damage
was done to the farm and to some nearby houses. A fire that
set alight two trees was extinguished.

The night of 12/13 December

Directional accuracy was poor in this single raid, which was
launched between 19.05 and 19.40 hours. Aircraft of II and III
Gruppen are known to have taken part. Fourteen missiles were
launched, of which five aborted and three got through. Six were
accounted for by AA fire, four over the sea. The results of the raid
were:

Abberton, Essex, 4 miles south-south-east of Colchester, at 19.30
hours. Hit by AA gunners, this bomb fell in a ploughed field
near Han Farm. Substantial damage resulted to the farm and
minor damage in the nearby village.

Fressingfield, Suffolk, 16 miles inland from Southwold, at 19.49
hours. Also hit by AA, this bug fell in a barley field east-south-
east of Rookery Farm. It caused damage to the farm and to Elm
Lodge, a bungalow, together with three other houses.
Fortunately there were no casualties. The ramjet unit was
recovered more or less intact.

Fringrinhoe, Essex, 3 miles south of Colchester.

Northaw, Hertfordshire, 2 miles east of Potters Bar.

Stansfield Abbotts, Hertfordshire, 4 miles west of Harlow.

The night of 17/18 December

This was a cold night with little wind and heavy cloud cover.
Visibility over the North Sea was poor. KG 53 mounted a major
effort after a four night pause, divided into two raids. The first was
the heaviest and commenced at about 03.45 hours, continuing at

short intervals until approximately 04.35 hours. After less than half an hour, at about 05.30 hours the second raid began, and it spluttered on until around 06.55 hours. The two attacks were despatched from separate launching zones, the second being further north. Because of the greater distance from the target, it was launched only 30 miles from the Norfolk coast, and was readily detected by CHL radar.

Pilot Officer K.D. Goodyear and his observer, Pilot Officer J. Burrowes, in Mosquito HK 263, coded VA-M of 125 Squadron under Hopton control, obtained three separate AI contacts and followed one of them, visually identifying a Heinkel 111 at 06.10 hours at 100 ft. They opened fire from a range of 200 yards, and saw a white glow and fire in the enemy's starboard engine. The slipstream from the enemy machine threw the Mosquito onto its back and contact was lost. A 'probable' was claimed but the Heinkel must only have been damaged for no loss was reported by the Germans.

Forty-five bombs were launched, of which sixteen aborted. Fifteen were shot down by AA over the sea and five over land, while fighters accounted for four over land. Only five got through unharmed. In both attacks they crossed the coast in the region south of Orford Ness and were exposed to AA gunfire from the strip. For example, 138 HAA Regiment, which engaged a number of robots from the second wave, alone expended 680 rounds of 'Bonzo' ammunition and claimed six bombs.

The first attack resulted in the following incidents:

Trimley St Mary, Suffolk, 3 miles north-west of Felixstowe, at 03.54 hours. This missile was shot down by AA and burst amongst trees at the south end of Painters Wood near Grimston Hall Farm. Minor damage was done to a post office, the farm and three houses. There were no casualties.

Orford, Suffolk, at 03.59 hours. An AA kill fell on Gedgrave Marshes, doing no damage.

Cretingham, Suffolk, 5 miles south-south-west of Framlingham, at 04.00 hours. A third AA victim exploded in a wheat field 200 yards from Stone House Farm, doing minor damage to the farm, Cretingham church and houses.

Stanmore, Middlesex, at 04.08 hours. A robot fell in a field off Glanleam Road, making a crater 35 × 8 ft and doing some damage to surrounding property.

Radlett, Hertfordshire, at 04.10 hours. Another bug fell just north-east of Kendal Hall and did extensive damage to it, its outhouses and surrounding cottage property, resulting in one serious shock casualty. Leaflets were found nearby, headed 'The Other Side No. 2'.

Newport, Essex, 3 miles south-south-west of Saffron Walden, at 04.10 hours. Warrant Officer W.O. Balam, on patrol in Tempest SD-N of 501 Squadron saw this diver coming from the Felixstowe direction, oddly at 6,000 ft, and climbing steadily at a speed of 300 mph, illuminated by searchlights. Climbing into position he fired three medium bursts at long range, after which the pulse jet appeared to burn brighter and the robot started losing height finally coming to earth in a ploughed field west of Whiteditch Farm. Only minor damage resulted.

Terrington Marshes, at the base of the Wash, at 04.25 hours. The Head Warden at Dersingham, Norfolk reported this fly as heading in that direction, after which it disappeared.

Shottisham, Suffolk, 9 miles east of Ipswich, at 04.30 hours. Two houses were significantly damaged when a doodlebug, hit by AA fire, exploded in a hedgerow south of Vale Farm.

Great Braxted, Essex, 4 miles north of Maldon, at 04.32 hours. Flying Officer R.C. Deleuze of 501 Squadron, saw a bomb coming inland from the coast at Felixstowe, illuminated by searchlights. He estimated its height at 450 ft and its speed at 320 mph. He gave it a long burst of fire, closing to 100 yards. Bits flew off it, and it went down steeply to explode in a stubble field at Kelvedon Hall Farm, doing some blast damage.

Skeffington, Leicestershire, 9 miles east of Leicester, at 04.40 hours. This missile set alarm bells ringing in defence circles. It was the only V weapon incident to occur in that county. One person was injured when farm buildings and a cottage at Glebe Farm were blasted. The breaking of an overhead electricity cable caused a local power failure.

Woolverstone, Suffolk, 4 miles south-south-east of Ipswich, at 04.48 hours. Claimed by the AA gunners, this bug fell in a beet field south of Woolverstone Hall on the side of the Orwell Estuary.

The second attack resulted in the following incidents:

Stebbing, Essex, 3 miles east-north-east of Great Dunmow, at 05.44 hours. Warrant Officer E. Wojczynski, in Tempest SD-G, saw a diver coming from the direction of Colchester at 1,800 ft and 340 mph. To ascertain the speed he made a three-quarter attack from the rear, firing three short bursts without result. He closed to 200 yards and aimed one long burst. The 'light went out' and the target started losing height to fall in a meadow south of Yew Tree Farm. There was some blast effect to Porter's Hall some 200 yards away.

Langford, Norfolk, 8 miles north of Thetford, at 06.03 hours. The ramjet of this fly cut out over Kimberley, causing it to glide down and explode in a plantation on a battle-training area. Some damage was done to Bodney Hall and to an acre of plantation.

Little Waltham, Essex, 4 miles north of Chelmsford, at 06.40 hours. Flight Lieutenant R.J. Lilwall, on patrol in Tempest SD-P, saw a diver coming from the Clacton area at 1,500 ft and 380 mph. He attacked from 10 degrees to port and above. After one short burst of fire strikes were observed and petrol vapour was seen to be leaking out of the robot. About thirty seconds later Lilwall observed a flash below him as the diver exploded in an orchard south of Drakes Farm, to which it did some blast damage.

The East Suffolk Civil Defence Authority logged this as the heaviest flying bomb attack on London to pass over the county.

The night of 22/23 December
After another four-night pause there was a token raid from 06.45 to 07.45 hours, launched from a zone some 50 miles off Lowestoft. Flight Lieutenant R.W. Leggett, with his observer, Flying Officer E.J. Midlane in Mosquito XVIII No. HK 247 of 125 Squadron, contacted a flying bomb. They turned in the direction of the launch aircraft and saw that a flare was being dropped. The Germans had experimented with the dropping of marking flares near the launching zone. Perhaps these experiments were still proceeding as late as December and the flare noted by the Mosquito crew was one of these.

As the dawn light improved they had a visual sighting which proved to be a Heinkel. The exhaust glow made it particularly visible and from 200 yards at 300 ft, they gave it a two-second burst of fire, seeing many strikes upon the fuselage and inboard of the port engine. As the Mosquito broke away to starboard the enemy was 'alight from stem to stern' and a large explosion was seen in the fore part before it hit the sea. It was from 7/KG 53, piloted by *Unteroffizier* Robert Rosch. Another Heinkel was lost by 9 *Staffel*, this time in an operational accident which killed the air gunner.

There were only eight launches this night, of which three were abortive and three shot down by AA over the sea. Those that got through and fell on land did so as follows:

Oldbury, Ightham, 4 miles east of Sevenoaks, at 07.10 hours. Five people were slightly injured when some seventy houses were damaged. Propaganda booklets from the fly entitled 'Signal' and leaflets headed 'V1 POW Post' were found near the impact site.

Shinfield, Berkshire, 3 miles south of Reading, at 07.58 hours. Only glass breakage occurred. *Signal* and 'V1 POW Post' leaflets, which are described in the next chapter, were discharged.

One of the carriers had a lucky escape; the ROC observer post at Southwold logged a diver 'launched from an aircraft 2 miles from this post'. This was confirmed by No. 5 AA Group which in its weekly intelligence summary, oddly reported:

Of the five [sic] flying bombs launched, one passed within range of the most southerly guns of Section A. This was plotted as a friendly fighter until it launched a flying bomb near the coast. YLDI saw the launching and had a fleeting glimpse of the aircraft as it banked away. HA sites also saw the flying bomb at the start of its run. The target was out of range of the LAA site and out of the firing arc of the HAA sites before visual engagement was possible.

The summary went on to report the next night's activities by KG 53:

23/24 December. In the early hours of Christmas Eve the enemy launched his first attack against the North Midlands. The enemy himself has said that the target was Manchester and whilst this may have been the intended target, in fact the 28 [sic] incidents were scattered over nine counties.

It was originally estimated that about 70 flying bombs were launched, but after a more detailed survey and taking into account the number of incidents over land, it is now considered that the number was about 40.

Main landfall was across the Humber mouth between Spurn and Mablethorpe. Humber guns engaged seven targets. Sites were not at that time specifically sited for an anti-diver role and were not holding Bonzo ammunition. There were no claims by AA or RAF.

The story behind this attack deserves a separate chapter.

CHAPTER ELEVEN

A Diversion to Manchester

Amongst the several RAF coastal radar stations to receive warning of enemy air activity over the North Sea in the early hours of Christmas Eve was that at Benacre Park, Wrentham, Lowestoft. On duty there as a radar operator was a Manchester man, F.J. Stott of Fallowfield.

Orders were given by the Women's Auxiliary Air Force (WAAF) shift supervisor to 'inch' the search into a narrow band to the north, and soon the blips of raiding KG 53 Heinkels appeared on the radar screen in a position some 40 or 50 miles seawards, off the northern part of the Lincolnshire coast. Some six or seven appeared within radar range, and in each case the separation of the blip into two indicated the launch of a V1 before the Heinkel dropped back to low level and disappeared from the screen. Corporal Stott was well aware that he was observing the launching of doodlebugs which might be directed at his home town.

Eight miles north-west of Skegness, a radar operator at Skendlebury, E.J.M. Jeffries and his colleagues 'were astounded at first to see several hostile tracks coming towards us and suddenly doubling in number. What was happening of course was that they were separating as the Heinkels turned for home while the doodlebugs continued towards land, very straight and extremely fast . . .'

The launchings were witnessed by several trawler crews and later reported. Skipper Gorringe of the trawler *Gurth*, fishing several miles south-east of the Dowsing Spar buoy, saw one successful and four or five failed launchings. Skipper Miller of the *Scout*, fishing fourteen miles north-east of 62B buoy, saw up to eighteen, mainly to the north-west of his position. He saw at least one bomb go into the sea.

The launches took place over a period of about an hour between 05.00 and 06.00 hours. None of the robots took more than about half an hour to complete its independent flight. Such was the importance that the Germans attached to this attack that they gave it a code name of its own – Operation Martha. Forty-five bombs were launched, of which fourteen aborted. None of the others was shot down. The seven which came within range of the AA guns of the Humber defences were engaged but no claims were made. It is possible, however, that one might have been winged, for a doodlebug flying up the Humber Estuary was seen by a civil defence worker, Mr K. May of Winterton. From Ferriby Sluice on

A map showing the impact locations of the missiles aimed at Manchester on 24 December. (Author's)

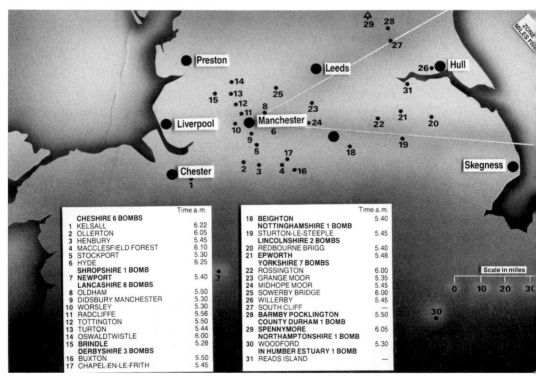

		Time a.m.
CHESHIRE 6 BOMBS		
1	KELSALL	6.22
2	OLLERTON	6.05
3	HENBURY	5.45
4	MACCLESFIELD FOREST	6.10
5	STOCKPORT	5.30
6	HYDE	6.25
SHROPSHIRE 1 BOMB		
7	NEWPORT	5.40
LANCASHIRE 8 BOMBS		
8	OLDHAM	5.50
9	DIDSBURY MANCHESTER	5.30
10	WORSLEY	5.30
11	RADCLIFFE	5.56
12	TOTTINGTON	5.50
13	TURTON	5.44
14	OSWALDTWISTLE	6.00
15	BRINDLE	5.28
DERBYSHIRE 3 BOMBS		
16	BUXTON	5.50
17	CHAPEL-EN-LE-FRITH	5.45

		Time a.m.
18	BEIGHTON	5.40
NOTTINGHAMSHIRE 1 BOMB		
19	STURTON-LE-STEEPLE	5.45
LINCOLNSHIRE 2 BOMBS		
20	REDBOURNE BRIGG	5.40
21	EPWORTH	5.48
YORKSHIRE 7 BOMBS		
22	ROSSINGTON	6.00
23	GRANGE MOOR	5.35
24	MIDHOPE MOOR	5.45
25	SOWERBY BRIDGE	6.00
26	WILLERBY	5.45
27	SOUTH CLIFF	—
28	BARMBY POCKLINGTON	5.50
COUNTY DURHAM 1 BOMB		
29	SPENNYMORE	6.05
NORTHAMPTONSHIRE 1 BOMB		
30	WOODFORD	5.30
IN HUMBER ESTUARY 1 BOMB		
31	READS ISLAND	—

the south bank he watched as it started a spiralling descent, and with its ramjet still running, plunged into the muddy water to the east of Reeds Island without exploding. It presumably lies there to this day. The limited distance flown by the bug may have been insufficient for its air log to have activated its electrical fuses, which may account for its not detonating. It did also have a mechanical fuse, but this may have failed due to the apparently shallow descent into water or soft mud.

The War Diary of 133 (Mixed) HAA Regiment at Hull records that one gun site, H 40, fired thirty rounds of 3.7 in and another, H 15, fired fourteen rounds of 40 mm ammunition against the divers.

From 68 Squadron, Flight Sergeant A. Bullus and his observer Flying Officer T. W. Edwards, in Mosquito XVII TA 389 under Orby radar control, were vectored onto a suspected target upon which they closed. They obtained a visual sighting of a Heinkel 111 and fired three two-second bursts.

The first at 200 ft struck the starboard wing root, the second at 100 ft the fuselage and the third at 50 ft the port engine and wing root. The target burst into flames, did an uncontrolled climbing turn to port and peeled off into the sea, where it was observed to be on fire for at least five minutes.

They expended 140 rounds of 20 mm cannon ammunition, gave the time of attack at 05.45 hours, reported good visibility with no cloud, and claimed one Heinkel destroyed.

Luftwaffe records show that the Heinkel was from 7/KG 53, piloted by *Unteroffizier* Herbert Neuber. The records also show that 7/KG 53 lost a second Heinkel in a crash landing at Leck airfield, in which one of the crew members was killed and another injured. This aircraft was attacked by Mosquito HK 247 of 125 Squadron. Hans Hoehler, who was the radio operator, graphically described his experience.

We climbed to launch height . . . As soon as we had launched the V1 we got hit by a hail of fire and were thrown from one side of the aircraft to the other and I felt something running down my back, with a pain in my neck . . .

His hand came away from a neck wound covered in blood but when he put a dressing on the wound, his flying suit held it in place. Luckily for the crew they were not attacked again.

Hoehler's main worry was that in their damaged condition the Heinkel would touch the waves on its low homeward flight. One member of the crew, *Unteroffizier* Gerhard Tanner was fatally wounded and had to be pulled from his seat. On the approach to landing at Leck the Heinkel's recognition lights were not working but the crew shot off emergency Very lights and made a crash landing, in which Hans was knocked unconscious. He was taken to hospital, where he was treated for concussion and a cannon shell splinter was removed from his neck. On discharge he was posted to an AA unit and did not fly again.

The ranging of the missiles, which German radio later announced were aimed at Manchester, was fairly accurate but the directional spread less so. Owing to the relatively crude construction there was a characteristic 'tail' of shortfalls from mechanical failure, and several wild directional strays.

Field Marshal Von Runstedt's large-scale counter-offensive out of the foggy Ardennes Forest in the early hours of 16 December 1944 came as a salutary shock, not only to the Allied command but to the British public. To many of them victory in Europe seemed almost within grasp. Despite the censorship it was obvious that there had been a setback in the period leading up to Christmas.

Those living in the northern industrial areas were in for a bigger shock still. With the Ardennes offensive still at its height a substantial air attack aimed at Manchester, which had been free of enemy air activity since August 1942, had not been expected. Dr Josef Goebbels's propaganda ministry, ever keen to put a 'spin' on any situation, announced the raid as 'the extension of our long-range weapons bombardment to Manchester in association with our western front offensive'.

Max Krull, a German radio commentator, said in a broadcast: 'We have begun using our V weapons against Manchester. The co-ordination of the land fighting with the action of long-range weapons, the stratospheric [sic] arm of which has been extended as far as Manchester, is becoming more and more conspicuous.'

On this raid an unusually high proportion – perhaps all – of the missiles are known to have carried small payloads of propaganda leaflets. They were of two types. One was a miniaturized version of the German magazine *Signal*, Volume 5, Number 17 of 1944. Printed in English, it was produced under the supervision of the German propaganda ministry, and had full-colour covers. In 8 × 6 inch format the front showed a clock face and the signs of the zodiac. This was intended to recall one of Hitler's speeches, indicating that he intended to go on fighting and that in this war Germany would not lay down its weapons as in 1918 but would continue the fight beyond the mythical midnight hour.

The second series of leaflets were single sheets printed on both sides in black and red on white paper, headed 'V1 POW Post'. At the top left-hand corner of each leaflet was an oblong in outline containing the words, 'The finder is requested to cut out or copy the letters printed here and to transmit them to the addresses so that they may receive them as early as possible. The letters are being sent through the Red Cross in the usual mail channel.'

Two formats were used, each 8 × 6 in, one landscape, the other portrait. Each leaflet had at its bottom right-hand corner one of a series of numbers from 1 to 6, each preceded by a V. The numbers indicated the content. Each contained three or four letters, both printed and reproduced in facsimile to prove their authenticity. These purported to come from British prisoners of war. They were in fact written in the German POW camp hospital at Stalag VIIA at Freising by POW patients. The addressee of each letter was clearly shown.

The Germans invited the prisoners to send an extra letter through Red Cross channels for Christmas, adding that the letters would be 'going by air'. So indeed they were but not in the way envisaged by the writers.

The Germans hoped to learn where the leaflets, which were scattered as the missile began its terminal dive, fell, and so to plot the accuracy of their aim. The finder would, they hoped, send the letter to the addressee, who would unsuspectingly write to the prisoner and hence to the German censors, saying where the letter had been found. This clever ruse failed, however, because the police had a standing instruction to gather in enemy leaflets. Further a discrete word from them to the addressees prevented any mention being made in return letters.

A positive slant to the German treatment of these particular prisoners was a useful secondary aspect of the exercise.

The propaganda leaflet ejector, when fitted to a flying bomb, was housed in the extreme rear of the fuselage. It contained a cardboard tube 30 in long and 2½ in in diameter. A small explosive charge activated by the air log which triggered the missile's dive threw the tube backwards from the missile. At the same time a length of fuse in the tube was lit, which ignited a small explosive charge within the tube when it was clear, releasing the leaflets.

Samples of enemy leaflets were treated by the Ministry of Home Security with a great deal of suspicion. The standing police instruction required that 'copies of enemy propaganda leaflets are sent by the police to a bacteriological laboratory'. A report from the

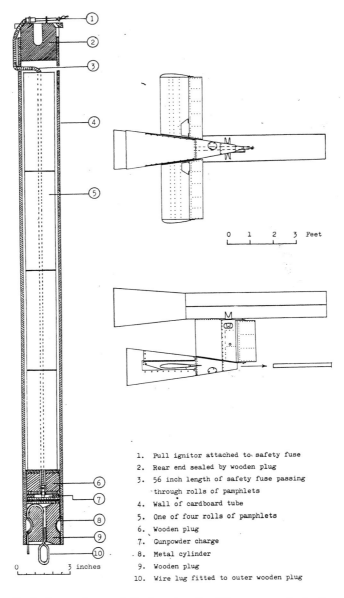

1.   Pull ignitor attached to safety fuse
2.   Rear end sealed by wooden plug
3.   56 inch length of safety fuse passing
     through rolls of pamphlets
4.   Wall of cardboard tube
5.   One of four rolls of pamphlets
6.   Wooden plug
7.   Gunpowder charge
8.   Metal cylinder
9.   Wooden plug
10. Wire lug fitted to outer wooden plug

The method of carrying and discharging the V1 propaganda leaflets. A cardboard cylinder stowed in the tail cone of the doodlebug was ejected by a small explosive charge and was disintegrated by another, releasing the leaflets. (Air Ministry)

Medical Research Council dated 23 January 1945 read: 'Representative samplings have been examined both by the cultural method and by animal inoculation. Tests did not disclose any evidence that the leaflets were contaminated with the germs of human or animal disease.'

V3 was the leaflet that was most widely distributed during the Manchester raid. It was found at Turton, Oswaldtwistle, Oldham, Tottington, Kelsal, Grange Moor, Rossington and Willerby. V4 appeared at Brindle, Ollerton, and Didsbury, V5 at Didsbury and South Cliffe, and V6 at Radcliffe, Worsley and Adswood. *Signal* magazine was found at Sturton le Steeple, Newport, Kelsal, Macclesfield Forest, Rossington and Epworth. The few V1 leaflets used are unlikely to have succeeded in either of their objectives to the slightest degree.

Owing to the distribution and number of incidents resulting from the Manchester raid it is convenient to list them by counties as well as chronologically.

Lancashire (8 bombs)

Gregson Lane, Brindle, 4 miles south-east of Preston, at 05.28 hours. Stonefield Cottages opposite Hewn Gate Farm were wrecked by a diver which fell in a field close behind. Three adults and a child were very lucky to escape without serious injury. A railway signal box was amongst the buildings which suffered slight damage.

Parrs Wood, Didsbury, 3 miles south of Manchester city centre, at 05.30 hours. The one missile to fall within the Manchester Civil Defence Area crossed Didsbury Road and the River Mersey before commencing its terminal dive. Taking a turn to the right it again crossed the river and exploded in a field of sprouts 50 yards from the north bank, damaging Underbank Farm at the bottom of Millgate Lane.

Worsley, 3 miles to the west of the city centre, again at 05.30 hours. A robot fell behind 18 Woodstock Drive. A child was killed and five adults injured when Nos. 16 and 18 were wrecked and other houses battered. On its flight this bug passed right over the city centre. A night nurse at Booth Hall Children's Hospital noticed the speed with which London evacuee children amongst her patients woke, recognizing the sound of the passing weapon. One nine-year-old boy sat upright in bed listening and then shouted, 'Doodlebugs – all under the bed.'

The V1 crater at Red Earth Farm, Turton, Lancashire, photographed in 1983. This crater was filled in and levelled shortly after the photograph was taken. (Author's photo)

Turton, Edgeworth, 3 miles north-east of Bolton, at 05.44 hours. A diver blew a crater in rough moorland above Red Earth Farm at the top of Plantation Road, but without effect.

Oldham at 05.50 hours. The worst tragedy of the raid occurred when a V1 made a direct hit on 115 Abbey Hills Road close to the junction with Warren Lane. Casualties were horrific – twenty-seven people killed and forty-nine injured. Some thirty-six houses were wrecked and seventy-three seriously damaged. Lesser effects spread over a 1 mile radius.

Tottington, 3 miles north-west of Bury, again at 05.50 hours. Simultaneously the second worst incident of the raid happened when a diver hit terraced houses in Chapel Street. In a memorial garden a plaque now records the names of the seven people who died in the incident.

This plaque in the Whitehead Memorial Garden at Tottington, Lancashire, commemorates the seven people who were killed here on 24 December 1944. (Author's photograph)

Radcliffe, 3 miles south-west of Bury, at 05.56 hours. The town narrowly escaped a similar catastrophe when a fly's motor cut out over the centre and it exploded at Allen's Green just beyond. A boat-building works was wrecked and lesser damage spread back as far as the town centre. Mercifully there were no serious casualties.

Oswaldtwistle, 3 miles east of Blackburn, at 06.00 hours. The last of the Lancashire bombs fell in a sloping meadow below Lower Westall Farm. Minor damage was done locally, mainly to farm property. The Oswaldtwistle police reported that 'a red light was seen in the sky which disappeared and a loud explosion followed'.

*Clearing the debris following the incident at Tottington, Lancashire.
Cottages in Chapel Street were wrecked and seven people were killed. The
site became the Whitehead Memorial Garden, given by the property
owners Mr and Mrs Whitehead in perpetuity to the people of Tottington
in commemoration of the victims.* (Librarian, Bury Local History Library)

Furnishings blown into the trees of St Ann's churchyard, Chapel Street, Tottington from the destroyed cottages make grotesque Christmas decorations for 1944. (Librarian, Bury Local History Library)

Buildings destroyed on the south side of Abbey Hills Road, Oldham, by the V1 explosion early on 24 December in which twenty-seven people were killed and forty-nine injured. This was the worst incident resulting from the Manchester raid. (Librarian, Metropolitan Borough of Oldham)

The church stands back from Chapel Street Tottington on a raised level but opposite the wrecked dwellings. The vicar was one of the first rescuers on the scene of the incident. Christmas day services were held in the church despite the damage. (Librarian, Borough of Bury)

The author with fragments of two of the V1s, Ollerton and Matley, which were found during his research. (Author)

The author with the tailpipe of the V1 which struck Macclesfield Forest, Cheshire, on 24 December 1944. (Author)

Cheshire (6 bombs)

Adswood, 2 miles south of Stockport, at 05.30 hours. An earth
bank behind 87 Garners Lane was struck by a diver which
spiralled down, wrecking the house and a bungalow next door.
The two occupants of No. 87 were seriously injured but the
resident of the bungalow escaped with lesser injuries. There
was other widespread property damage.

Three miles west of Macclesfield, behind Bluebell Wood, only 500
yards from Henbury Hall, at 05.44 hours. The Hall was

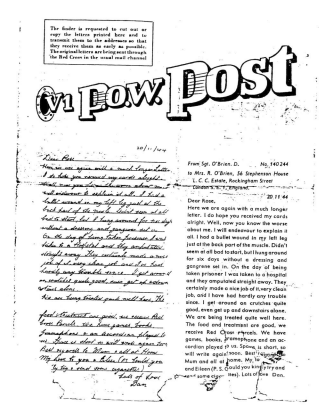

*Leaflet number V1/3 of the series 'V1 POW Post'. This leaflet was
picked up at Kelsal, Cheshire on 24 December 1944. The missile which
carried it penetrated further west than any other V weapon and fell only
7 miles from the tidewater of the west coast of England. (Author's leaflet)*

Westwood Farm, Matley, Hyde, Cheshire before its destruction by a V1 in the early hours of 24 December. (Mrs Betty McKeown)

Westwood Farm, Matley, Hyde, Cheshire, after its destruction by V1 in the early hours of 24 December. Two people were killed here and three severely injured. (Mrs Betty McKeown)

protected from more than minor damage by the great trees of the wood.

Ollerton, 2 miles east of Knutsford in a field of Manor Farm on Seven Sisters Lane, at 06.05 hours. A crater was blown. Despite some damage to the farm, the only casualty was a farm worker sleeping in one of the outbuildings, and his injuries were slight.

Five Ashes, 3 miles east of Macclesfield on the Buxton road, at 06.10 hours. Beyond the hamlet, in the area known as Macclesfield Forest, a crater, still visible to this day, was blown between Crooked Farm Yard and Clough House Farm, both of which suffered material damage. One person was seriously injured.

Kelsal, 7 miles east of Chester, at 06.22 hours. The most westerly V1 to impact during the raid fell at Lower Farm. Minor damage was done but there were no casualties.

The water-filled flying bomb crater on Midhope Moor between Manchester and Sheffield, photographed in 1993. (Author's photograph)

Matley on the A628 2 miles east of Hyde, at 06.25 hours. The last of the Cheshire missiles was the most deadly, hitting a tree in front of the farmhouse at Westwood Farm. The farm was wrecked and a nearby public house with other property damaged. The farmer and his wife, who were in the bedroom nearest the explosion escaped with serious injuries, as did their daughter. The son and mother-in-law, who were sleeping at the back of the house, were both killed by the blast.

Yorkshire (7 bombs)

Dumsteeples Farm, Grange Moor, 5 miles east of Huddersfield, at 05.35 hours. A bomb blew in doors and windows of council houses and even knocked the bottles and glasses off the shelves of a pub. The one casualty suffered a cut foot from flying glass.
Midhope Moor, 5 miles south-west of Penistone, at 05.45 hours. A fly failed to clear the Pennine crests and struck the moorland slopes of Margery Hill, exhausting its energy on the moss.
Willerby, in the western outskirts of Hull, again at 05.45 hours. A bug burst in a field close to Springhead water pumping station.

The original size of the crater at Hob Tor, Doveholes was measured as 33 ft across and 4½ ft deep. (Frank Leyland)

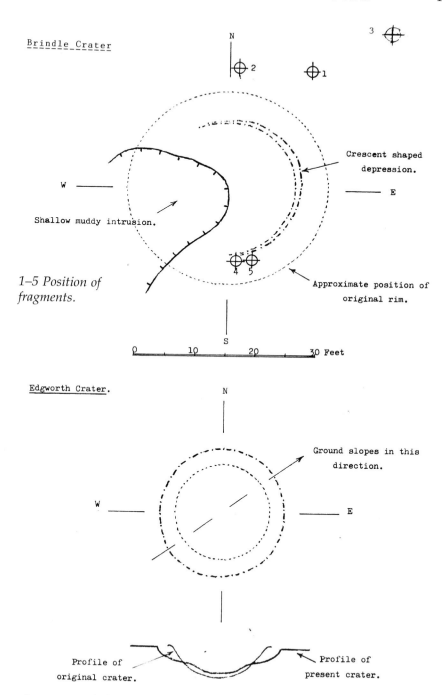

Brindle Crater

N

3

2

1

Crescent shaped
depression.

W

E

Shallow muddy intrusion.

1–5 *Position of fragments.*

4 5

Approximate position of
original rim.

S

0   10   20   30 Feet

Edgworth Crater.

N

Ground slopes in this
direction.

W

E

Profile of
original crater.

Profile of
present crater.

Surveys carried out in the 1980s of two surviving V1 craters in the Manchester region. (Frank Leyland)

There was one slight casualty and windows were broken over a wide area.

Barmby Moor airfield, 10 miles south-east of York, at 05.50 hours. A bug exploded on the north-west boundary, doing substantial damage in the village. A Halifax bomber of 102 Squadron, parked at dispersal, was knocked about.

Rossington Hall on the Great North Road, 5 miles south of Doncaster, at 06.00 hours. A missile did superficial harm to a farm and to the lodge. It brought down overhead telephone wires, causing a temporary disruption of communications.

Hubberton Green, Sowerby Bridge, 4 miles south-west of Halifax, again at 06.00 hours. Little Tootill Farm was wrecked by a bomb which also damaged Tootill End Farm and did superficial damage in Hubberton Green hamlet. The lady occupant of Little Tootill Farm suffered permanent injuries.

Bunnyhill Farm, 15 miles west-north-west of Hull. A V1 struck a ditch bank ½ mile from the farm. Minor damage was done mainly to the hamlets of North and South Cliffe.

Derbyshire (3 bombs)

Beighton, 6 miles south-east of Sheffield, at 05.40 hours. A robot impacted on grassland at Field Farm. There were no casualties but damage was done to the farm and to 150 buildings in Killamarsh and district.

Doveholes, 4 miles north of Buxton, at 05.45 hours. A V1 which may have failed to clear the Pennine crest, impacted in the rock and peat of Hob Tor, Black Edge.

Burbage Moor, 2 miles from Buxton, at 05.50 hours. A missile made a crater which can still be traced near a disused railway tunnel entrance.

Lincolnshire (2 bombs)

Redbourne, 8 miles south-east of Scunthorpe, at 05.40 hours. A bomb came down in a stubble field 350 yards east of Woofham Hill Farm. Some fabric damage was done to the farm and to its neighbour Paradise Farm. Luckily there were no casualties.

Epworth, 8 miles south-west of Scunthorpe, at 05.48 hours. A robot fell in Clarke's beet field, 150 yards south-east of a mill. The mill suffered, as did forty houses.

Nottinghamshire (1 bomb)

Sturton le Steeple, 5 miles south-west of Gainsborough. A diver cratered a ploughed field off Littleborough Road, 2 miles west of the River Trent.

County Durham (1 bomb)

One missile went wildly astray and flew north-west. It fell on the Tudhoe Colliery cricket field at Charles Road, a mile north of Spennymoor at 06.05 hours. The vicarage and seventeen other houses were seriously damaged. Some others suffered lesser damage, as did the church. A man and three women were seriously injured.

Shropshire (1 bomb)

A bug impacted in a field at Middle Farm, Chetwynd, a mile east of Newport at 05.30 hours, after gliding for a considerable distance. The police at Stafford reported that its engine cut out over that town. It retained its axis of flight; it must have been despatched from the southern part of the launching zone. Sixteen plate glass windows were broken in Newport.

Northamptonshire (1 bomb)

Another wild stray exploded in a field at Grange Farm, Woodford, a mile south-west of Thrapston, at 05.30 hours, causing superficial damage to buildings but no casualties.

There was a spread of 170 miles between the northernmost bomb at Spennymoor and the southernmost at Woodford. Excluding these two and the one at Newport, however, the spread was approximately 40 miles north to south and over land 100 miles east to west.

Of the thirty-one missiles that crossed the coast, nineteen fell within a 30 mile radius of Manchester, fifteen within a 20 mile radius, six within 10 miles. The mean point of impact (MPI) lay 2 miles to the east of the city.

The raid on Manchester arguably marked the peak of the air-launched V1 campaign. It circumvented the concentrated defensive shield protecting London and all the non-abortive missiles ran their course, with perhaps one exception.

On 17 January 1945 the Ministry of Home Security issued a letter to all civil defence regions, headed 'Attacks on areas which have had an immunity for some time'. Betraying some official alarm, it read:

The recent flying bomb attack on the North, which may well be repeated and may be extended to other areas, has emphasized the importance of ensuring that the Civil Defence Services are kept up on a state of operational efficiency . . . many Wardens' Posts have been shut and in some areas Wardens' Posts are only open for short periods in the early evening . . . All personnel must be definitely informed of their obligations to turn out on an alert, or on enemy action occurring . . . and of the consequences which may follow failure to report for duty.

The letter was probably instigated by Mr (later Sir) Hartley Shawcross, the Regional Civil Defence Commissioner for No. 10 Region, based in Manchester. His report on the events of 24 December was in some respects critical of the way in which the Oldham incident had been handled. He commented that it was too large to be controlled by one incident officer, and that the civil defence organization in the region needed overhauling.

Despite the warning, hope was allowed to triumph over caution. The feeling was abroad by then that the end of the war in Europe could not be long delayed and there was a disinclination in the north to take air raids seriously any more.

CHAPTER TWELVE

January 1945 – A Matter of Spirit

The year opened with a major setback for the *Luftwaffe*. At first light, in Operation *Bodenplatz*, 800 of its fighters launched an attack on Allied airfields in Holland, Belgium and France in a bid to cripple the Tactical Air Force on the ground. The operation not only failed in its objective, it also cost the Germans dearly in terms of their least readily available resource – aviation fuel.

Since Romania had become Germany's ally in 1941 the oilfields at Ploesti, north of Bucharest, had been crucial to the German war effort, but from August 1943 they had been subject to increasingly heavy, if intermittent, Allied bombing raids. The Soviet troops occupied them a year later.

Synthetic oil production was Germany's only alternative. It was based on her extensive deposits of bituminous and brown coal, from which oil was manufactured by two processes: the Bergius hydrogeneration and the Fischer-Tropsch. Both required complicated equipment, but by the first quarter of 1944 some 47 per cent of the Reich's oil products were being synthesized; for aviation fuel the proportion was even higher.

By May 1944 the Allied air forces were powerful enough to take on the task of destroying the 150 oil-manufacturing plants under German control, which were scattered widely across Europe, but were concentrated in the Ruhr area, near to deposits of bituminous coal and in central Germany, near to brown coal. Two plants in particular, one at Leuna, south-west of Berlin, and the other at Politz, north-east of the capital, were large producers.

An offensive by aircraft based in Britain began on 12 May when 935 heavy bombers of the Eighth USAAF attacked oil targets in Germany and Czechoslovakia. The offensive was eased during the immediate preparations for the D-Day landings but resumed soon afterwards.

So successful was the offensive that it soon had a crippling effect on *Luftwaffe* operations. Some 175,000 tonnes of aviation fuel were produced in April 1944, but this was down to 156,000 tonnes in May, 53,000 tonnes in June, 29,000 tonnes in July, 16,000 tonnes in August and in September a mere 7,000 tonnes. Throughout the summer and into the autumn the *Luftwaffe* kept going on its reserves, some 580,000 tonnes in April which had sunk to 180,000 tonnes at the end of September.

The offensive was then eased in favour of bombing other targets. This failure to maintain the pressure resulted in some recovery in synthetic oil production. Production of aviation spirit rose to 18,000 tonnes in October and 39,000 tonnes in November. The bombing was resumed in the middle of December and this time the effect was terminal. By March 1945 the remaining fuel stocks were almost exhausted.

With the new year only three days old KG 53 received a fuel allocation for its first attack of 1945, and sufficient for an operation on a significant scale.

The night of 3/4 January 1945
This was to be the last major raid carried out by the air-launch Heinkels. It was divided into two extended attacks, so close together that the total effect was that of a single operation over the period from about 18.30 to 20.25 hours, making it the longest air-launched V1 raid.

KG 53 lost three of its Heinkels on the operation, apparently due to accidents since no claims were lodged by defenders. No. 3 *Staffel* lost one, piloted by *Feldwebel* Heinz Kowalsi, who perished with all his crew. No. 7 *Staffel* lost two, in each of which one crew member was killed. Forty-five launches were made, of which seventeen aborted and nineteen fell victim to AA fire, eleven over the sea. Those that fell on land did so with the following results:

> Aldeburgh, Suffolk, on the coast, at 18.35 hours. No casualties were caused, but extensive damage was done to one house and less to another twelve when a diver shot down by AA exploded in a ploughed field west of Aldeburgh Hall.

Ellough, Suffolk, 7 miles south-south-west of Lowestoft, at 18.45 hours. Claimed by AA gunners, this bug clipped a flagpole on the parish church during its shallow descent. It came to earth with a bang in an open field, from where its blast damaged the church and some thirteen houses. There were no casualties.

Doepham Green, Norfolk, 14 miles west-south-west of Norwich, at 18.57 hours. This bomb detonated near the south-western corner of a USAAF base, damaging five cottages but causing no casualties.

Goose Green, Tendring, Essex, 9 miles west-south-west of Harwich, at 19.00 hours. Damage was done to farm property. A 10 ton stack of straw was set on fire and destroyed despite the best efforts of the NFS. This fly too was claimed by the AA gunners.

Bredfield, Suffolk, 2 miles north of Woodbridge, at 19.02 hours. Another kill claimed by AA, this bomb burst amongst trees at White House Lodge, which was demolished. Lesser damage was done to other premises. Two people were seriously injured.

High Ongar, Essex, 9 miles west of Chelmsford at 19.12 hours. Casualties and serious damage were avoided when a diver burst on ploughed land at Waterend Farm. A crater 17 × 5 ft was reported.

Sutton, Norfolk, 12 miles north-west of Yarmouth, at 19.43 hours. Disabled by AA, this missile fell as an unexploded bomb (UXB). It dived nose first into a soft dyke and partly buried itself. Petrol escaped and caught fire but even this failed to explode it, probably because of water in the dyke. Digging it out proved impractical and the bomb-disposal team leader finally decided to blow it up *in situ*. This lifted a lot of earth but fortunately did little damage.

Hopton, Suffolk, 8 miles east-south-east of Thetford, at 19.50 hours. An impact cratered a field 250 yards south of Jay Lane damaging some thirteen houses. This bug also fell to the AA gunners.

Hempnall, Norfolk, 19 miles inland from Lowestoft, at 20.00 hours. Shot down by AA fire this robot fell in a field at Rookery Farm, Topcroft. There were no casualties but minor damage was done to some twenty houses. USAAF personnel removed the wreckage. An unusually large crater was reported, measuring 35 ft across and 16 ft deep.

Lewisham, London, at 20.14 hours. After an alert at 20.10 hours, the missile fell on allotments 200 ft east of Ewhurst Road,

south-east of its junction with Manwood Road. Severe damage
was done to four houses and a crater was left, reported as 38
ft by 9 ft deep.

Langham, Essex, 5 miles north of Colchester, at 20.25 hours. The
robot, hit by AA fire, struck the north side of a lane from
Maltings Farm about a mile east of Boxted Heath, leaving a
crater 24 × 4 ft in clay.

North Weald, Essex, 14 miles north-west of Central London, at
20.34 hours. A detached bungalow was wrecked and made a
crater 27 ft wide and 9 ft deep in clay soil was made by a missile
which landed in a ploughed field south-west of Canes Farm.

Heydon, Cambridgeshire, 4 miles south-west of Duxford.

Godmanchester, Huntingdonshire.

Moulsoe, Buckinghamshire, 2 miles south-east of Newport
Pagnall.

Shelley, Essex, a mile north of Chipping Ongar.

The final missile is untraced but may have been an unreported air
burst.

The night of 5/6 January

There was a single raid this night, between 22.10 and 22.25 hours.
It was accurate but costly. Headquarters Flight lost a Heinkel on the
ground to an intruder attack. The *staffeln* suffered too. No. 7 lost
one plane, piloted by *Leutnant* Kurt Neuber, who was posted as
missing with his whole crew. No. 9 *Staffel* lost one of its aircraft,
shot down near its base by intruder action. *Hauptman* Siegfried
Jessen, the *staffel* commander, and his crew perished. The same
staffel lost another Heinkel in an accident, in which two crew
members lost their lives.

Ten missiles were launched, of which half aborted. Two were
downed by AA, one over the sea. The following incidents were
recorded:

Braintree, Essex, at 22.25 hours. Shot down by AA, this bomb
exploded in a ploughed field ½ mile west of Wickham Hall,
without doing significant damage.

Beckenham, London, at 22.26 hours. Eleven people were killed
and twenty-two seriously injured when, only three minutes
after the alert, a diver fell to the rear of two-storeyed terraced
houses on Burnhill Road. Twelve were destroyed and four
others seriously damaged. A surface air-raid shelter 25 ft from
the point of impact was shifted by 14 in.

Lambeth, London, at 22.29 hours. An explosion at the rear of houses on the south side of Fentiman Road, west from its junction with Carroun Road, killed fourteen people and seriously injured thirty-six. Two houses were destroyed and another twelve suffered lesser harm. These included two semi-detached cottages and some three-storey terraced old properties.

Wanstead, London, at 22.45 hours. A direct hit was made on 355 Roding Lane. Two semi-detached and three terraced houses were wrecked and others seriously damaged.

The night of 12/13 January

It was perhaps only a single *staffel* of KG 53 which launched this token raid. Two Mosquito crews of 68 Squadron made contact, but both lost it before any conclusive engagement. Five launches were made, of which two aborted. Only one evaded the British defences. The following incidents occurred:

Chislehurst, Sidcup, London, at 06.05 hours. A bungalow was badly damaged when a diver exploded in a field east-south-east of the junction of North Cray Road and Barton Road.

Great Holland, Essex, west of Frinton, at 06.09 hours. Shot down by AA beside the golf links, this bug caused no harm.

Chapel St Andrew, Suffolk, 3 miles west of Orford, at 06.52 hours. AA fire felled this doodlebug, which failed to detonate when it came down in the yard of Capel Green Farm. Captain H.J. Hunt RE, who was in charge of the bomb-disposal operation, arrived at the site to find that the bomb was submerged in a cesspool to a depth of 6 ft, with only the propulsion unit visible. The mess had to be cleared from the shoulders of the missile to enable X-ray equipment to be used before the fuses were removed. As fast as his men dug down, the muck oozed back on them. A tractor and a cable were borrowed from a nearby RAF emergency landing ground. Placing the tractor behind the farmhouse, they ran the cable round a tree, securing one end to the body of the V1. Taking up the slack, the bomb-disposal team lay down under cover on the far side of the tractor and the strain was taken up. So great was the suction of the mire that the tractor merely dug itself in. In desperation they had to give it a running tug, then the cable snapped. Another, heavier cable was obtained from the airfield and this time the missile was pulled clear and its fuses removed.

The night of 13/14 January

This turned out to be the last air-launched flying-bomb raid, and lasted from 01.35 to 02.05 hours. Twenty-five bombs were launched, of which ten aborted and seven were shot down by AA (five over the sea) and one by a fighter. Seven got through. Reported incidents were:

Orpington, London, at 01.50 hours. This fly fell in an orchard east of Layhams Road near its junction with North Pole Road. Waits Cottage, a two-storeyed brick house was blasted. Oddly a single leaflet headed 'The Other Side' was recovered in Gravesend and is presumed to have come from this missile or another which impacted in Orpington later. The unreported leaflets which must have fallen with it most likely fell into private hands.

Southwark, London, at 01.55 hours. After an alert at 01.50 hours a fly made a direct hit on two-storeyed brick terraced homes on the east side of Horseman Street, near to its junction with Bethwin Road. Eight were demolished and another thirteen badly damaged. Ten people were killed and seventeen seriously injured. Nearby railway arches were blasted but the heavy, solid, structure remained intact and railway services were barely interrupted.

Mitcham, London, at 01.56 hours. Two sets of railway tracks were broken and railway services stopped when a missile fell on an embankment near the south end of Caesar's Walk on the south side of Hatton Gardens. Telephone wires were brought down and extensive damage done to local property.

Epping, Essex, 1 mile south-west of North Weald aerodrome, at 02.00 hours. A diver burst on contact with trees in a corner of Wintry Wood.

Orpington, London, at 02.01 hours. A second missile here made a direct hit on 102/104 Court Road. The houses were modern semi-detached properties. Five were wrecked and another badly affected.

Southminster, Essex, 8 miles south-east of Maldon, at 02.07 hours. Hit by AA, this fly was an air burst a mile south of Scrubwater Hall.

Hornsey, London, at 02.12 hours. Finsbury Park was cratered and adjacent properties blasted.

Enfield, London, at 02.20 hours. South-south-west of the King James and Tinker Inn a diver burst in trees on the edge of Whitewebbs Park doing damage to property.

Southwold, Suffolk. AA fire exploded a bomb over the town. This injured a soldier and did superficial damage to two churches, 230 houses and seventy-nine shops and businesses.

North Cray, Kent, 3 miles east of Sidcup. This fly fell to the guns of Squadron Leader A.T. Langdon-Downs in Tempest SD-K of 501 Squadron. It was a fitting finale to the squadron's successes in its anti-air-launched-V1 role. The unit remained at Bradwell Bay until 3 March 1945 when it was posted to Hunsdon to the north of London.

The fuel limitations imposed on KG 53 meant that the unit achieved only about fifty more sorties (750) than did III/KG 3 (700) in the air-launching role.

CHAPTER THIRTEEN

March 1945 – Ramps Again

The cessation of air launching operations did not quite spell the end of the V1 campaign. There were still a 'last few shots' left in the locker, which were to constitute Phase 3, the last phase of Operation *Rumplekammer*.

An extended-range version of V1 was at the planning stage as early at June 1944. The basic design remained the same but to lighten the structure plywood was used in the construction of the wings and warhead casing. To increase the range a lighter warhead was fitted and myrol used for the explosive filling. The specific gravity of this mixture was 25 per cent lower than the usual amatol, but it had a similar destructive effect.

The balance of the missile was maintained by placing the reduced warhead further forward in a fuselage extension welded to the front of the fuel tank. The forward part of the extension was strengthened by a 5 in wide steel band. This modification of the nose section increased the overall length of the missile to about 30 ft.

After testing it must have been found that, even with the warhead placed further forward, the bomb was still slightly tail heavy. The remedy was to fill the space between the warhead and the fuel tank (which straddled the mainspar at the centre of gravity) with a load consisting of twenty-three 1 kg (2.2 lb) incendiary bombs clustered in a vertical cylinder to hold them steady. The nose of each incendiary bomb fitted into a hole perforated in a circular steel plate 12 in in diameter. The fins of the incendiaries were also secured to prevent any movement in flight. The steel retaining plate was probably jettisoned by a small explosive charge when the missile

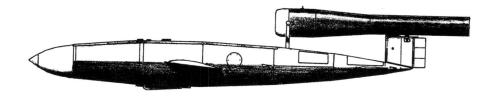

1. Experimental flying bomb tested at Peenemünde.

2. Standard production version of the flying bomb.

3. Extended range version with reduced warhead.

The three types of unmanned V1 flying bomb. The length and other differences are clearly evident. (Frank Leyland)

reached the end of its intended flight, which would coincide with the tipping of the asymmetric spoilers under the tail plane, thus releasing the incendiaries as the robot tipped into its terminal spiraling dive.

Enlargements of the fuel tank and compressed air containers in the modified missile increased its range from 150 to 200 miles, sufficient for it to reach London from ramps in German-occupied territory in western Holland.

FZG 76 Flying Bomb (Fi 103 A/Re 1 Extended Range)

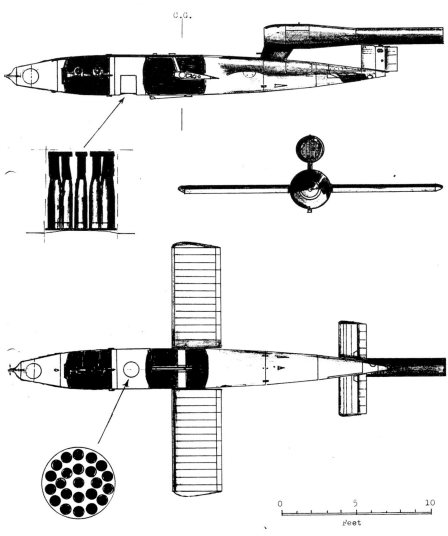

The incendiary-bomb-carrying arrangement of the extended range V1
which renewed the ramp launch attack in March 1945. (Frank Leyland)

Fragments of some of the doodlebugs fired into Belgium in February 1945 showed that they were in part constructed of lighter materials and adapted for longer-range flight. The conclusion was drawn that they might be capable of reaching London, and on 26 February Allied air reconnaissance photographs of the most likely areas for such ramps showed that two launching sites were being constructed, one at Ypenburg near the Hague, the other at Vlaardingen six miles west of Rotterdam. In fact the Germans constructed a third ramp near the Delft canal at Delft, which began firing on 9 March, but the British were unaware of it until later.

The *Luftwaffe*'s Operation Gisela, a long-planned and, for its time, large-scale piloted intruder raid over Britain, directed primarily against bomber airfields and their returning aircraft, was carried out on the night of 3/4 March. The previous day flying-bomb attacks were resumed from the ramps at Ypenburg and Vlaardingen.

The *Daily Telegraph* of Monday, 4 March reported: 'The Germans during the weekend resumed attacks on this country with flying bomb and piloted aircraft. It is believed that flying bombs that crossed the coast have come from land launching sites much more distant than any previously used.'

Mr E.C. Comber, in *Memoirs of a Spotter*, recorded his memories of the opening of this phase of the V1 campaign.

A report from the Alarm Controller at 16.00 hours on the following afternoon [Saturday, 3 March] stated that flying bombs had been over Suffolk and at the time of speaking three more were passing just south of Ipswich. This was the first time for several weeks. The bearing taken seemed to indicate the Isle of Sylt or north-west Germany as possible launching sites. Explosions were heard at 18.05 hours, with further reports of V1s south of the observation post at 21.12 hours.

In the first few hours of the raid thirteen flying bombs were picked up on radar but only seven came within range of the defences, six of which were shot down into the sea. The seventh reached the London Civil Defence Region and came down in the Borough of Bermondsey. On 3 March seven bombs again survived to come within range of the coastal guns, and three were shot down into the sea. A fourth was hit and exploded just above the cliffs at Walton, Essex.

To meet this new threat, Air Marshal Hill and General Pile reinforced the defences between the Isle of Sheppey and Orford Ness by transferring ninety-six heavy guns from the northerly part of the strip and adding a number of batteries then under training. By Tuesday, 6 March, they were taking up their positions.

Home-based fighter units were also rearranged to meet the threat. Air Marshal Hill earmarked six Mustang squadrons for operations against the bombs in daylight and arranged that their engines should be specially boosted. Three of these squadrons reequipped with Meteor jet fighters borrowed from the Second Tactical Air Force (TAF) on the Continent and these, plus 616 Squadron which already had Meteors, were to operate between the coastal guns and London. The other three Mustang squadrons would carry out over-sea patrols. A direct link was established with the radar stations of the Second Tactical Air Force in Belgium to give warning of the approach of divers from the general direction of the Scheldt.

As early as 2 March, 83 Squadron of 2 TAF attacked the two known launching sites. Although extensive damage was caused in the area of each, the ramps were unharmed. Not until late March did air attacks finally knock out the launching sites at Ypenburg and Vlaardingen. The third site at Delft remained undetected and continued launches right up until the cessation of the campaign on 29 March.

The three sites between them launched some 275 missiles, but only 160 came close enough to be detected on UK-based radar. Thirty-one of these evaded the British defences, thirteen of which reached London.

Friday, 2 March
Thirteen missiles were detected, but six failed to reach the British defences and six were shot down by AA over the sea. The sole evader landed in Bermondsey, London.

Saturday, 3 March
Nine were detected, of which two failed to reach the defences. Four were shot down by AA, three over the sea. Of those that fell on land, the results were as follows:

> Frinton, Essex, at 04.56 hours. A V1 air burst over Walton Cliffs was caused by AA fire. Incendiary bombs were found amongst the wreckage.
> Cuffley, 14 miles north of central London.
> Stapleford, Hertfordshire, 23 miles north of central London.
> Wood Green, London.

Sunday, 4 March
Three were detected, and all three got through, falling at:

> Redbourne, 5 miles south of Luton.
> Chertsey, Surrey, south-south-west of central London.
> Camberwell, London.

Monday, 5 March
Ten were detected, four of which did not trouble the defences. Two were shot down by AA, one over the sea. The remainder fell at:

> Foulness Island, Essex, shot down by AA fire.
> Barnet, London, 11 miles north-west of the city centre.
> Barking, London, 9 miles east of the city centre.
> Bermondsey, London, 3 miles south-east of the city centre.
> Enfield, London, 10 miles north of the city centre.

Tuesday, 6 March
Eight were detected by UK radar, of which three did not reach the defences. AA fire accounted for three (one over the sea) and a fighter for one. Four that fell on land were as follows:

> Billericay, Essex. Shot down by AA at Langdon, 2 miles to the north.
> Shelley, Essex. Shot down by a fighter a mile north of Chipping Ongar.
> Wade, Kent. Fell at St Nicholas, 6 miles west-south-west of Margate.
> Sandon, Essex. An AA kill fell 3 miles east-south-east of Chelmsford.

Thursday, 8 March
UK radar detected three, of which two were shot down by AA over the sea. The remaining one was shot down over land, falling at Tillingham, Essex, 3 miles south of Bradwell Bay.

Wednesday, 14 March
Six were detected by UK radar, of which five were shot down by AA over the sea. The remaining one fell at Ealing, London.

Thursday, 15 March
Four were detected, of which one failed to reach the British defences. The remainder were shot down by AA over the sea.

Friday, 16 March
Only one was detected. It exploded at 05.35 hours at Moreland Avenue, Dartford, Kent, killing four people and injuring twenty-seven. Over 450 houses were damaged.

Saturday, 17 March
UK radar detected five, of which four fell victim to AA. The evader penetrated to Somersham, 8 miles north-east of Huntingdon, at 02.55 hours.

Sunday, 18 March
The radar picked up two, of which one failed to reach the defences and the other was shot down by AA over the sea.

Monday, 19 March
Nine were picked up on the UK radar, but four failed to reach the defences and one was downed by AA over the sea. The ones that got through resulted in the following incidents:

   Harlow, Essex, at Great Parndon on the western edge, at 05.47
      hours.
   Shipbourne, Kent, 5 miles south-east of Sevenoaks, at 08.12 hours.
   Sutton Valence, Kent, 5 miles south-east of Maidstone, at 09.14
      hours.
   Thornham Parva, Suffolk, 5 miles south of Diss, at 09.16 hours.
      Minor damage was done to a farm, and twenty-one incendiary
      bombs were found.

Tuesday, 20 March
Only two were picked up on the radar, both were shot down by AA over the sea.

Wednesday, 21 March
UK radar detected three, all of which were shot down by AA, one over the sea and two over land. These fell at Foulness Island, Essex and Little Oakley, Essex, 3 miles south-west of Harwich. The one which fell into the sea did so off Felixstowe at 23.52 hours.

Thursday, 22 March
Twelve were detected, of which two did not reach the defences and nine were shot down by AA over the sea. One was shot down by AA over the land and fell next to Frinton golf course at Great Holland, Essex. Burnt-out incendiary bombs were found at the site.

Friday, 23 March
The radar detected six, of which three did not reach the defences. The remainder fell as follows:

Thorpe Park, Essex, between Southend and Shoeburyness, at 05.05 hours. Shot down by AA fire.
Eltham, Kent, 8 miles east-south-east of central London. There was serious damage to two houses, less harm to 150 houses and a railway station.
Chicksands, Bedfordshire.

Saturday, 24 March
UK radar picked up four. One was brought down by a fighter over the sea, and three fell at follows:

Ardeley, Hertfordshire, 4 miles east-north-east of Stevenage, at 03.07 hours.
Marden Ash, Chipping Ongar, Essex.
Paddington, London.

Sunday, 25 March
Fourteen were detected by UK radar, but only two got through. Four did not reach the defences, seven were shot down by AA, four over the sea, and one fell to a fighter. Incidents reported were:

Bradwell on Sea, Essex. This one fell to AA fire south of the Blackwater Estuary.
Tillingham, Essex, south of Bradwell. This also fell to AA fire.
Leysdown on Sea, Kent. AA fire also accounted for this one on the Isle of Sheppey.
Buttsbury, Essex, 4 miles south-east of Chelmsford. This was the fighter kill.
East Grinstead, Sussex. This evader fell at Lowdells Lane, seriously injuring two people and another six slightly. Some fifty shops and houses were damaged.
Dagenham, London. The other evader fell here.

Monday, 26 March

UK radar picked up nine, but two failed to reach the defences. AA guns accounted for another four (three over the sea), and a fighter for one. Just two evaded the defences. The following incidents were reported:

> Great Bromley, Essex, 5 miles south-east of Colchester. This one was claimed by AA.
> Berners Roding, Essex, 5 miles west-north-west of Chelmsford. This fly fell to a fighter.
> Chelsham, Surrey, 5 miles south-east of Croydon
> Orpington, London.

Tuesday, 27 March

Ten were picked up on the radar, but nine were shot down by AA fire over the sea. The sole evader landed at North Cray, Kent, 3 miles south-west of Dartford and 14 miles from central London.

Wednesday, 28 March

Fifteen were detected. Eleven fell to AA fire over the sea, and two over land. The incidents involving the four that fell on land were:

> Great Holland, Essex, at 00.04 hours. The fly fell to AA fire.
> Foulness Island, Essex. Another AA kill.
> Waltham Holy Cross, London, 18 miles north of central London.
> Chislehurst, London, 12 miles south-east of central London.

Thursday, 29 March

On this final raid, British radar picked up twelve bombs. Three did not reach the defences, and four were shot down by AA over the sea. Another four were shot down over land, and just one evaded the AA's destruction. The following incidents occurred:

> Datchworth, Hertfordshire, 3 miles south-east of Stevenage, at 08.56 hours. This evader damaged six houses.
> Iwade, Kent, 3 miles north of Sittingbourne, at 10.00 hours. This missile fell to AA fire.
> Great Wigborough, Essex, 7 miles south-south-west of Colchester. This fly also fell victim to AA.
> Little Oakley, Essex, 4 miles south-south-west of Harwich. This third victim of the AA gunners damaged thirty-one houses, two farms and a church.
> Great Wakering, Essex, 1 mile north of Shoeburyness. This was another kill for the AA.

At 12.43 hours a flying bomb shot down into the sea off Orford Ness, Suffolk, by the AA gunners was the last V1 to approach the British Isles and it is a fitting tribute to the gunners of AA Command that it should be their achievement.

The potential flexibility of V1 spread alarm beyond Europe. The *Daily Express* on 9 January 1945 reported a threat to New York from V bombs fired from U-boats.

This city was warned today that it will probably be attacked by flying bombs within the next thirty to sixty days.

The warning came from Admiral Jones Ingram C-in-C of the US Atlantic Fleet, who said that he had been authorized at a meeting of the General Staff to assure the public that both army and navy were well prepared to ward off the expected attacks. If such an attempt were made, Ingram told reporters, 'It would probably be limited to ten or twelve bombs. These would not be of the blockbuster type.

'Less explosive – they might strike a building and destroy it but casualties would be nothing like the people of London are suffering because the weapons would carry more fuel and less explosive.

'There are three ways that the flying bombs would be launched against this or other American cities – by airplane, submarine or surface ship.'

Ingram said that steps had been taken to ward off attacks. Presumably they are largely naval because he admitted that his visit to the unnamed east coast port where he gave his warning was connected with these preparations. The Germans, he said, would have at least 300 [sic] submarines in the Atlantic. Six or eight would be needed to attack New York and they might take up positions within 100 miles of it. Admiral Ingram will on Wednesday go to sea aboard his flagship to put into operation his plans for defence against the robots.

ARP [air-raid precaution] units have been alerted along America's east coast for several weeks. The public have been told that there is no reason to become alarmed but that, at the same time, they should be ready. Ingram said that the purpose of such attacks as described would be largely political.

The German propaganda leaflet 'The Other Side No. 1' under its headline 'V1, Those Last Few Shots', dropped from air-launched flying bombs during November 1944 ended its article with the words, 'According to Mr Sandys V1 had a range of 160 miles. How far distant is the German front line from London today? It looks as if Mr Sandys was wrong once again. V1 you see is a secret weapon and it has more than one secret. Mr Sandys does not know what they are.'

Admiral Ingram's warning surely indicated a secret too far.

Air launched V1 Operations against London, 9 July– 5 September 1944

Date	Radar Estimated Launches	Approached Coast	Came Over land	Shot Down Over Land By AA	By Fighter	Reached London
July						
9/10	9	8	8			3
18/19	18	11	10			9
19/20	24	14	13			10
21/22	19	10	10	1		2
23/24	30	11	11			5
24/25	30	11	10			6
25/26	11	9	9			3
26/27	8					
30/31	22	14	10	1		8
31/	5					
August						
2/3	15	7	6	1		5
21/22	22	8	7			3
29/30	24	7	7			2
30/31	21	4	4			
September						
4/5	19	10	9		2	
Totals	277	124	114	3	2	56

An estimated ninety flying bombs were air launched against London in late June and early July 1944. Southampton was attacked on four seperate nights between 10 and 15 July, during which about ninety flying bombs were launched. After the first two weeks of July the air-launch unit III/KG3 moved from French to Dutch bases.

APPENDIX II

Air-launched Flying-bomb Operations, Phase 2, 15 September 1944– 15 January 1945

Authoritative statistics relating to the air-launched flying bombs over the period 15 September 1944–14 January 1945 are to be found in the semi-official account *The Defence of the United Kingdom* by Basil Collier.

Equally authoritative statistics are to be found in the report of Air Marshal Sir Roderic Hill to the Secretary of State for Air, published as a supplement to the *London Gazette* of Tuesday, 19 October 1948 under the heading 'Air Operations by the Air Defence of Great Britain and Fighter Command in connection with the German Flying Bomb and Rocket Offensives 1944–1945.

There are some variations between these, and between them and this study, as follows:

	Collier	Hill	This Study
Launches from aircraft	1200 (est.)	608	1075 (inc. Manchester)
Flying bombs destroyed by the defences	403	406 (engaged)	403
Eluded defences	235	205	267 (inc. Manchester)
Reached London	66	66	63
Reached Manchester			1

Launches reported by the German authorities for the period September to 13 December are given as:

September	177 bombs on 13 nights (includes those of 4/5 Sept.)
October	282 bombs on 21 nights
November	316 bombs on 13 nights
1–13 December	90 bombs on 6 nights.
	865

Summary

Air launched V1 operations against London – Phase 2
15 September 1944–14 January 1945

Night of	No. of flying bombs launched	Aborted launches	Shot down oversea By AA	By fighter	Shot down overland By fighter	Evaded defences	Reached London	Incident locations region
September								
15/16	15	7	2		2	4	2	Felstead, Essex. Saffron Walden, Essex. Barking, London. Woolwich, London. Latchington, Essex. Cliffe, Kent.
17/18	6	3			1	2	1	Canewdon, Essex. Thorpe, Essex. Regents Park, London.
18/19	12	4				8	1	Toppersfield, Essex, Tan Vats, Lincolnshire, Mitcham, London. Tollesbury, Essex. Hornchurch, Essex. (2) Romford, Essex, Battlesbridge, Essex.
19/20	15	7			1	7	1	Little Baddow, Essex. Rushden, Herts. Lawford, Essex. Dunmow, Essex. Bethnal Green, London. Essendon, Herts. Cockfield, Suffolk. Maldon, Essex.
20/21	19	8	1		1	9	4	Chediston, Suffolk. Richmond, London. Poplar, London. Codicote, Herts. Wandsworth, London. Waltham Holy Cross, London. Great Totham, Essex. Felixstowe, Suffolk. Hatfield, Herts. Hacheston, Suffolk.

Night of	No. of flying bombs launched	Aborted launches	Shot down oversea		Shot down overland		Evaded defences	Reached London	Incident locations region
			By AA	By fighter	By AA	By fighter			
22/23	12	7	1		1		3	1	Bradwell, Essex. Enfield, London. Little Heath, Herts. Hatfield, Herts.
23/24	15	7		1	1		6		Thaxted, Essex. Braughing, Herts. Swainsthorpe, Norfolk. Framsden, Suffolk. Codicote, Herts. Pirton, Herts. Burwell, Cambs.
24/25	16	11				1	4	2	Hessett, West Suffolk. Tilbury Juxta Clare, Essex. Chertsey, Surrey. Ridgeway Enfield, London. Chigwell, London.
25/26	10	6	2		1		1		Henham, Essex. Great Bromley, Essex.
26/27	7	3			2		2	1	Sible Heddingham, Essex. Ardleigh, Essex. Edmonton, London. Maldon, Essex.
28/29	11	4			1	1	5		Chelmondiston, Suffolk. Saffron Waldon, Essex. Barrow, Suffolk. Edwardstone, Suffolk. Barnston, Essex. Bygrave, Hertfordshire. Sutton, Cambs.
29/30	20	11	1		2		6		Baythorpe End, Essex. Walthamstow, London. Shudy Camps, Cambs. Wixoe, Suffolk. Tiptree, Essex. Nazeing, Essex. Meopham, Kent. Rudgwick, Sussex.
Total	158	78	7	1	11	4	57	13	

Night of	No. of flying bombs launched	Aborted launches	Shot down oversea By AA	By fighter	Shot down overland By AA	By fighter	Evaded defences	Reached London	Incident locations region
October									
5/6	11	1	1		3	1	5	3	Stutton, Suffolk. Shearing, Essex. Romford, Essex. Surbiton, London. Colchester, Essex. Leatherhead, Surrey. Edgeware, London. Heston, London. Chertsey, Surrey.
6/7	12	4	1	1	2	1	3	2	Woodhouse Ferrers, Essex. Orpington, London. City of London. Latchingdon, Essex. Weybridge, Surrey. Mayland, Essex.
7/8	11	2	1	2	2	2	2	1	Cheshunt, London. Little Yeldham, Essex. Greenstead, Essex. Purfleet, Essex. Sutton at Hone, Kent. Fawkenham, Kent.
8/9	15	5	3		3		4	1	Marks Tay, Essex. Assington, Essex. Wangford, Suffolk. Sudbury, Suffolk. Hornsey, London. Saxmundham, Suffolk. Thwaite St Mary, Suffolk.
9/10	11	3	3		1		4	2	Thurleigh, Bedford. Billericay, Essex. Hampstead Heath, London. Potters Bar, London. Hatfield, Herts.
11/12	4	2	1			1			Felsted, Essex.
12/13	17	7	2		2	2	4	2	Salcott, Essex. River Blackwater. Harlington, Beds. Stratford St Andrew, Suffolk. Navestock, Essex. Great Coggeshall, Essex. Wanstead, London. Friern Barnet, London.

Night of	No. of flying bombs launched	Aborted launches	Shot down oversea		Shot down overland		Evaded defences	Reached London	Incident locations region
			By AA	By fighter	By AA	By fighter			
13/14	18	4	4			1	9	1	Great Fransham, Norfolk. Cressingham, Norfolk. Latimer, Suffolk. Maulden Wood, Bedford. Stretton, Rutland. Ranson Moor, Cambs. Worlington, Suffolk. Dagenham, London. Beazley End, Essex. Great Burstead, Essex.
14/15	22	7	3	2	5	2	3	2	Southwold, Suffolk. Lowestoft, Suffolk. Hopton, Suffolk. Steeple, Essex. Camberwell, London. Dovercourt, Essex. Waltham Cross, London. Tillingham, Essex.
15/16	19	5	6		3		5	1	Northaw, Herts. Nayland, Suffolk. Luddesdown, Kent. Shopland, Essex. Beachy Head, Sussex. Manea, Cambs. Benacre, Suffolk. Trimley St Mary, Suffolk. Chislehurst, London. Noblesgreen, Essex.
16/17	7	3	1		1	1	1		Kirby Le Soken, Essex. Ongar, Essex. Dartford, Kent.
17/18	11	3	5		2	1			Kirby Le Soken, Essex. Dengie, Essex. Grays Thurrock, Essex.
18/19	19	5	6		6		2	1	Frinton, Essex. Ipswich, Suffolk. Thorrington, Essex. Weeley, Essex. Edmonton, London. Oulton Broad, Suffolk. Thurlton, Norfolk. Alpheton, Suffolk.

Night of	No. of flying bombs launched	Aborted launches	Shot down oversea		Shot down overland		Evaded defences	Reached London	Incident locations region
			By AA	By fighter	By AA	By fighter			
19/20	25	6	5	5	5	3	1	1	Orford, Suffolk. Dengie, Essex. Ramsey, Essex. Debden, Essex. Great Bentley, Essex. Fyfield, Essex. Stoney Point, Essex. Potters Bar, London. Hatfield, Herts.
20/21	9	3	2		3		1		Great Wakering, Essex. Barking, Suffolk. Dovercourt, Essex. Skippers Island, Essex.
21/22	9	2	1			3	3	3	Rivenhall, Essex. Rayleigh, Essex. Cheshunt, London. Navestock, Essex. Chingford, London. Hackney, London.
23/24	19	5	3		3	2	6	1	Grays, Essex. Lamarsh, Essex. Worth, Sussex. Woolwich, London. St Mary Hoo, Kent. Dunston, Essex. Snape, Suffolk. Bedlam, Sussex. Hartlip, Kent. Grays, Essex. Ashtead, Surrey.
24/25	13	3	4	2	1	1	2		Hartfield, Sussex. Detling, Kent. Latchingdon, Essex. Laindon, Essex.
25/26	12	3	2	2	1	2	2	1	Martlesham, Suffolk. Boughton, Kent. Downe, Kent. Margaretting, Essex. Richmond, London.

Night of	No. of flying bombs launched	Aborted launches	Shot down oversea		Shot down overland		Evaded defences	Reached London	Incident locations region
			By AA	By fighter	By AA	By fighter			
28/29	9	4	2		1	1	1	1	Hollesley, Suffolk. Danbury, Essex. Banstead, London.
30/31	10	3	2		1	1	3	3	Couldson, London. Sudbourne, Suffolk. West Ham, London, Great Wigborough, Essex. Richmond Park, London.
Total	283	80	58	14	45	25	61	26	
November 4/5	23	11	6		3	2	1		Debden, Essex. Breckles, Norfolk. Brentwood, Essex. Ongar, Essex. Radwinter, Essex. Southminster, Essex.
5/6	27	15	2		1		9		Winchelsea, Sussex. Shoreham, Sussex. Wisborough Green, Sussex. Crawley, Sussex. Steyning, Sussex. Overflew Kent and Sussex. Telescombe, Sussex. Aldeburgh, Suffolk. Kennington, Kent. Frant, Sussex.
6/7	27	9	12		5		1		Westleton, Suffolk. Tendering, Essex. Foulness Island, Essex. Kelsale, Suffolk. Great Oakley, Essex. Bapchild, Kent.

Night of	No. of flying bombs launched	Aborted launches	Shot down oversea		Shot down overland		Evaded defences	Reached London	Incident locations region
			By AA	By fighter	By AA	By fighter			
8/9	32	13	5	2	3	2	7		Stockbury, Kent. Detling, Kent. Northbourne, Kent. Rochester, Kent. Newington, Kent. Leadon Roding, Essex. Swanscombe, Kent. Four Elms, Kent. Meopham, Kent. Ivy Hatch, Kent. South Stifford, Essex. Frant, Sussex.
9/10	29	11	9	1	3	1	4	1	Walthamstow, London. Lullingtone, Sussex. Throwley, Kent. East Grinstead, Sussex. Dengie, Essex. Ramsey, Essex. Brentwood, Essex. Minster, Kent.
10/11	48	15	21	1	4	3	4	2	Wymondham, Norfolk. Writtle, Essex. Ufford, Suffolk. Shotley, Suffolk. Ash, Kent. Orford, Suffolk. Clacton, Essex. Hunsdon, Herts. Dagenham, London. Great Warley, Essex. Beckenham, London.
13/14	21	11	5		3		2	2	Hockley, Essex. Eastchurch, Kent. Thames Haven, Essex. Sible Headingham, Essex. Cooling, Kent.

Night of	No. of flying bombs launched	Aborted launches	Shot down oversea		Shot down overland		Evaded defences	Reached London	Incident locations region
			By AA	By fighter	By AA	By fighter			
14/15	37	13	7		6		11	6	Middleton, Suffolk. Falkenham, Suffolk. Glenham, Suffolk. Cuxton, Kent. Martlesham, Suffolk. Frien Barnet, London. Berkhamsted, Herts. Rayleigh, Essex. Felstead, Essex. Croydon, London. Pembury, Kent. Saint Pancras, London. Little Bentley, Essex. Fyfield, Essex. Sutton, London. Surbiton, London, Bethnal Green, London.
17/18	23	13	5		2		3		Orsett, Essex. Hadleigh, Essex. Rayleigh, Essex. Fristling, Essex. Buntingford, Herts.
19/20	13	3	7		2		1		Carlton Colville, Suffolk. Copford, Essex. Brickendon, Herts.
22/23	10	3	3		2	1	1		Great Burstead, Essex. Wherstead, Suffolk. Sudbourne, Suffolk. Harlow, Essex.
23/24	16	5	6		3	1	1		Colchester, Essex. Dovercourt, Essex. Kirby Cross, Essex.
24/25	10	6	2		1		1	1	Springfield, Essex. Boxford, Essex. Great Bentley, Essex. Hampstead, London.
Total	316	128	90	4	37	11	46	10	

Night of	No. of flying bombs launched	Aborted launches	Shot down oversea		Shot down overland		Evaded defences	Reached London	Incident locations region
			By AA	By fighter	By AA	By fighter			
December									
4/5	11	3	7				1		East Malling, Kent.
5/6	15	8	2		1	2	2	1	Takeley, Essex. Manuden, Essex. Chignall, Essex. Walthamstow, London. Swale, Kent.
7/8	21	8	9		2	1	1		East Hornon, Essex. Foulness Island, Essex. Chelmsford, Essex. West Mersea, Essex.
10/11	15	7	2		3		3	1	Walton, Essex. Chelmondiston, Suffolk. Levington, Suffolk. Tottenham, London. Kirby Le Soken, Essex. Great Barford, Beds.
11/12	14	7	1		2		4	1	Hopton, Norfolk. Monkton Barn, Essex. Burnham, Essex. Hanningfield, Essex. Beddington, London. Rainham, Essex.
12/13	14	5	4		2		3		Abberton, Essex. Fressingham, Suffolk. Fingringhoe, Essex. Northaw, Herts, Stanstead Abbots, Herts.
17/18	45	16	15		5	4	5		Trimley St Mary, Suffolk. Orford, Suffolk. Cretingham, Suffolk. Stanmore, Middx. Radlett, Herts. Newport, Essex. Shottisham, Suffolk. Great Braxted, Essex. Skeffinton, Leics. Woolverstone, Suffolk. Stebbing, Essex. Langford, Norfolk. Little Waltham, Essex. Terrington, Norfolk.
22/23	8	3	3				2		Shinfield, Berks. Oldbury Ightham, Kent.

Raid directed at Manchester

Night of	No. of flying bombs launched	Aborted launches	Shot down oversea By AA	By fighter	Shot down overland By AA	By fighter	Evaded defences	Reached Manchester region	Incident locations
23/24	45	14					31	1	Lancashire – Brindle, Didsbury, Worsley, Turton, Oldham, Tottington, Radcliffe, Oswaldtwistle. Cheshire – Adswood, Henbury, Ollerton, Five Ashes, Kelsal, Matley. Yorkshire - Grange Moor, Midhope Moor, Willerby, Barmby Moor, Rossington, Hubberton Green, South Cliffe. Derbyshire – Beighton, Doveholes, Burbage Moor Nottinghamshire – Sturton Le Steeple. Durham – Tudhoe Shropshire – Chetwynd Northamptonshire – Woodford Humber Estuary – Reads Island Lincolnshire – Redbourne, Epworth

Night of	No. of flying bombs launched	Aborted launches	Shot down oversea		Shot down overland		Evaded defences	Reached London	Incident locations region
			By AA	By fighter	By AA	By fighter			
January 1945									
3/4	45	17	11	8			9	1	Aldeburgh, Suffolk. Ellough, Suffolk. Deopham Green, Norfolk. Goose Green, Essex. Bradfield, Suffolk. High Ongar, Essex. Sutton, Norfolk. Hopton, Suffolk. Topcroft, Norfolk. Lewisham, London. Langham, Essex. North Weald, Essex. Heydon, Cambs. Godmanchester, Hunts. Moulsoe, Bucks. Shelley, Essex. Hempnall, Norfolk
5/6	10	5	1	1			3	3	Braintree, Essex. Beckenham, London. Lambeth, London. Wanstead, London.
12/13	5	2	2	2		1	1	1	Chislehurst, London. Great Holland, Essex. Capel St Andrew, Suffolk.
13/14	25	10	5	2		1	7	6	Orpington, London. Southwark, London. Mitcham, London. London. Epping, Essex. Orpington, London. Southminster, Essex. Hornsey, London. Enfield, London. Southwold, Suffolk. North Cray, Kent.
Total	85	34	17	13		1	20	11	

Air launched V1 operations – Phase 2 – Against London

	No. of flying bombs launched	Aborted launches	Shot down oversea		Shot down overland		Evaded defences	Reached London	Incident locations region
			By AA	By fighter	By AA	By fighter			
September	158	78	7	1	11	4	57	13	
October	283	80	58	14	45	25	61	26	
November	316	128	90	4	37	11	46	10	
December	188	71	43		15	7	52	3 (+ 1 Manchester)	
January	85	34	17		13	1	20	11	
Total	1030	391	215	19	121	48	236	63	

Luftwaffe Ranks and Approximate RAF Equivalent

Officers

Generalfeldmarshsal	Marshal of the RAF
Generaloberst	Air Chief Marshal
General der Flieger	Air Marshal
Generalleutnant	Air Vice-Marshal
Generalmajor	Air Commodore
Oberst	Group Captain
Major	Squadron Leader
Hauptmann	Flight Lieutenant
Oberleutnant	Flying Officer
Leutnant	Pilot Officer

Non commissioned Officers

Stabsfeldwebel	Warrant Officer
Oberfeldwebel	Flight Sergeant
Feldwebel	Sergeant
Unteroffizier	Corporal

Officer Candidates

Fahnrich
Fahnenjunker

Other Ranks

Obergefreiter	Leading Aircraftsman
Gefreiter	Aircraftsman First Class
Flieger	Aircraftsman

Technical Data

Air-launched flying bomb

Length of fuselage	6.65 metres (21ft 9in)
Wingspan	5.33 metres (17ft 6in)
Overall length including tailpipe	8.32 metres (27ft 3⁄in)
Warhead weight	850 kg (1,874 lb)
Maximum diameter of fuselage	83.8cm (2ft 9in)
Launch weight	2,200 kg (4,851 lb)
Electrical fuses	Az 106 and Z17BM
Mechanical fuse	Kz 80A
Maximum range	150 miles

Heinkel III flying-bomb carrier variants

The Heinkel III mark intended for flying bomb carrier duties was the H-22 and this was to have two Jumo 213 E-1 engines of 1,750 hp each. The engine was, however, late in its development and unavailable. Some H-21 Heinkel IIIs on the production line, also designed for use with the Jumo 213, were temporarily fitted with Jumo 211 F-2 engines of 1,350 hp each. A few of these were converted to H-22 configuration.

The great majority of the flying-bomb carrier Heinkel IIIs employed were, however, simply adapted H-16 or H-20 types and these were treated in *Luftwaffe* records under these old designations.

Crew	5
Length	16.4 metres (53 ft)
Height	4 metres (13ft 1½ in)
Wingspan	22.6 metres (74 ft 2 in)
Wing area	87.6 sq. metres (942.6 sq ft)
Weight empty	10,500 kg (23,157 lb)
Weight loaded	15,930 kg (35,126 lb)
Armament	1 x MG 131, 4 x MG 81Z

APPENDIX V

KG 53 In Training

Report dated 14 October 1944, regarding the performance of the Fi 103, when air-launched by crews of III/KG 53 in training at Karlshagen:

Date	Successful launch	Abortive launch
4-10-44	14	7
5-10-44	3	2
7-10-44	9	2
8-10-44	8	2
9-10-44	4	–
11-10-44	16	4
	54	17

Launching failure rate: 23.94 per cent

The investigation and evaluation of the performance of the missiles, resulted in the following information:

1. Twelve flying bombs failed immediately after being launched from the carrier aircraft.
2. Five flying bombs ended their flights prematurely, shortly after being air-launched. Reasons for failures not known.
3. Five flying bombs crashed before the scheduled termination of flights. The reasons for these failures are not known.
4. There were five cases where the engines failed to develop full power.
5. There were three crashes about which no conclusions could be reached at all.
6. One flying bomb was judged to have crashed due to a ground-handling failure.

In all, forty flying bombs performed satisfactorily, attaining ranges of 75 km (46.1 miles) to 85 km (52.8 miles). However, as all the flying bombs had been programmed for a range of 60 km (37.3 miles), the excess represented a considerable margin of error.

The reduced ranges were ensured not only by a small fuel load, but also by a reduction in the amount of compressed air carried on these training flights.

Although the flights of the missiles were studied with some interest, the emphasis was more on the actual technique of air-launching at this time and the performance of the crews in training.

KG 53 Organization Diagram, December 1944

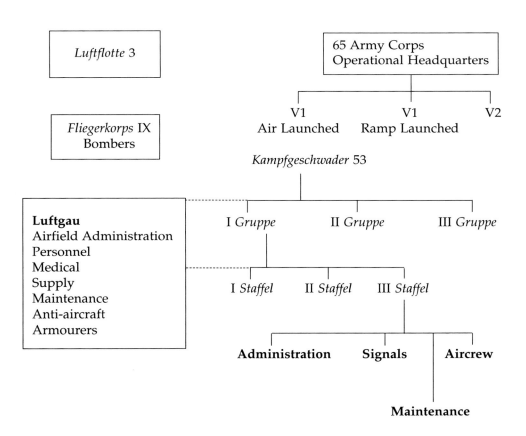

KG 53 Command Structure from 15 October 1944

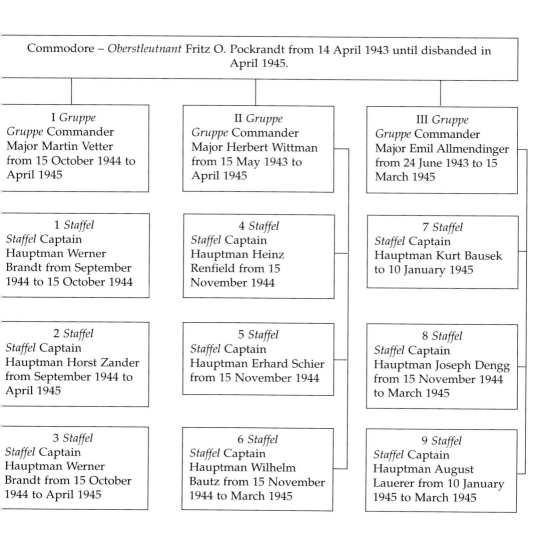

Commodore – *Oberstleutnant* Fritz O. Pockrandt from 14 April 1943 until disbanded in April 1945.

I *Gruppe*	**II *Gruppe***	**III *Gruppe***
Gruppe Commander Major Martin Vetter from 15 October 1944 to April 1945	*Gruppe* Commander Major Herbert Wittman from 15 May 1943 to April 1945	*Gruppe* Commander Major Emil Allmendinger from 24 June 1943 to 15 March 1945
1 *Staffel* *Staffel* Captain Hauptman Werner Brandt from September 1944 to 15 October 1944	**4 *Staffel*** *Staffel* Captain Hauptman Heinz Renfield from 15 November 1944	**7 *Staffel*** *Staffel* Captain Hauptman Kurt Bausek to 10 January 1945
2 *Staffel* *Staffel* Captain Hauptman Horst Zander from September 1944 to April 1945	**5 *Staffel*** *Staffel* Captain Hauptman Erhard Schier from 15 November 1944	**8 *Staffel*** *Staffel* Captain Hauptman Joseph Dengg from 15 November 1944 to March 1945
3 *Staffel* *Staffel* Captain Hauptman Werner Brandt from 15 October 1944 to April 1945	**6 *Staffel*** *Staffel* Captain Hauptman Wilhelm Bautz from 15 November 1944 to March 1945	**9 *Staffel*** *Staffel* Captain Hauptman August Lauerer from 10 January 1945 to March 1945

9 Anti-Aircraft Group Deployment Within the Gun Strip at 18 November 1944

5 AA Brigade

138 HAA Regiment: 419 battery, Lambert's Grove,
  Orford (3 sites); 437 Battery, Thorpeness Overmere (3 sites);
438 Battery, Aldeburgh area (3 sites)
119 HAA Regiment; 372 Battery, Thorpeness (3 sites);
422 Independent Battery, near Orford (3 sites); 433
  Independent Battery, Aldeburgh (3 sites)
135 LAA Regiment: 477 Battery, Aldeburgh (2 sites);
450 Battery, Leiston (2 sites); 432/131 Battery, Aldeburgh (1 site).

37 AA Brigade

142 (M) Regiment: 488 Battery, Bradwell (1 site); 261 Battery,
  Great Baddow (1 site); 433 Battery, Stanford le Hope (1 site);
  196 Independent Rocket Battery, Colchester; 211 Independent
  Rocket Battery, Chelmsford.

40 AA Brigade

126 HAA Regiment, Clacton area; 423 Battery, Ramsey – Dovercourt (3 sites); 425 Battery, Harwich (2 sites); 426 Battery, Thorpe le Soken (3 sites); 431 Battery, Clacton (2 sites)

136 Regiment, Walton area: 182 Battery (3 sites); 409 Battery (2 sites); 432 Battery (2 sites); 468 Battery, Felixstowe (2 sites)

150 (M) HAA Regiment: 489 Battery, Felixstowe (2 sites); 492 Battery, Shotley (3 sites); 515 Battery, C3/C4, Jaywick/Frinton (3 sites); 456 Battery, Ipswich/Nacton, H12 and H18 sites; one troop of 439 Independent HAA Battery attached to 492 Battery at H5, Lt Oakley

19 LAA Regiment, Frinton area: 221 Battery, Clacton (1 site); 263 Battery, Walton (3 sites); 294 Battery, K 16, Frinton; 431/131 Battery, Harwich

81 LAA Regiment, Parkeston area: 199 Battery (2 sites); One troop, 261 at Felixstowe

171 Independent Rocket Battery, Frinton

50 Searchlight Regiment; 401, 402 and 403 Batteries at Frinton

56 Brigade

32 Searchlight Regiment: 328, 329 and 300 Batteries at Woodbridge, Saxmundham and Manningtree respectively; 453/64 Battery attached, Ipswich–Belstead

43 Detached Brigade

32 Searchlight Regiment attached, 314/58 Battery, Frinton.

57 Brigade

188 Independent Rocket Battery, Halesworth

48 Searchlight Regiment; 391 and 392 Batteries, Southwold 437/132 LAA Battery, Leiston.

102 AA Brigade, Ipswich area.

378 Independent HAA Battery, Ipswich

134 LAA Regiment: 192, 275 and 457 Batteries around Eyke also 1514 Regiment with 449, 472 and 478 Batteries

28 Searchlight Regiment, Bawdsey area: 309, 312 and 438 Batteries.

53 Searchlight Regiment: with searchlight Batteries 408 (Ipswich), 409 (Colchester) and 410 (Harwich) – Construction units.

RAF Fighter Squadrons Deployed Against the Air-launched Flying-bomb Raids

Squadron	Coded	Aircraft Type	Station	Dates	Primary Role
25	ZK	Mosquito	Coltishall, near Norwich	Dec 1943–27 Oct 44	Engage carrier aircraft
			Castle Camps, near Steeple Bumpstead, Cambs.	27 Oct 44–July 1945	
68	VM	Mosquito XIX	Castle Camps	23 June–27 Oct 44	Interception of VI between launching zone and coast until mid-November; also sought carrier aircraft
			Coltishall	27 Oct–Feb 45	
125	VA	Mosquito XV11	Detachment at Bradwell Bay, Essex	31 July–18 Oct 44	Engage carrier aircraft
			Coltishall	18 Oct 44–April 45	
456	RX	Mosquito	Ford, near Arundel	Feb–Dec 44	Guard southern flank

Squadron	Coded	Aircraft Type	Station	Dates	Primary Role
			Church Fenton, Yorks	1 Jan 45–16 Mar 45	
501	SD	Tempest V	Bradwell Bay	22 Sept 44–3 Mar 45	Engage divers that escaped coastal AA guns
307	RX	Mosquito XII	Church Fenton, with detachment at Coltishall	6 May 44–27 Jan 45	Guard Northern flank
96	ZJ	Mosquito XII	Castle Camps Ford	27 Jan–May 45 20 Jun–24 Sept 44	Guard Southern flank
406	HU	Mosquito	Manston	27 Nov 44–14 Jan 45	Guard Southern Flank and Intruder work

The Fighter Interception Development Unit (Fighter Interception Development Squadron as it became, on 18 October 1944), coded ZQ, engaged in experimental methods of interception of the carrier Heinkels.

No. 409 Squadron equipped with Mosquito XIII aircraft operated from continental airfields starting in August 1944, and it claimed the first carrier to be shot down.

APPENDIX X

Carrier Aircraft of III/KG 3 and KG 53 Shot Down by Night Fighters

Date	Squadron	Aircraft	Crew	
25 September	409	Mosquito	–	Mosquito force landed at Lille/Vendeville
29 September	25	Mosquito HK 357	W. Cdr. L.J. Mitchell F. Lt. D.L. Cox	45 miles east of Yarmouth
29 September	25			a second victory to the same crew
5 October	25	Mosquito HK 239	F. Lt. J.F.R. Jones F. O. H. Skinner	
6 October	25	Mosquito HK 257	F. Lt. E.E. Marshall F. O. C.A. Allen	
25 October	125	Mosquito HK 310	F.O. W.A. Beadle F.O. R.A. Pargeter	Heinkel from 2/KG 53. Pilot O/FW O. Hammerle
30 October	125	Mosquito HK 325	F. Lt. L.W.G. Gill F. Lt. D.A. Haigh	Heinkel from 4/KG 53. Pilot F/w T. Warwas

Date	Squadron	Aircraft	Crew	
4 November	FIDS	Beaufighter V 5365	S. Ldr. F.O. J. Howard –Williams F.O Macrae	Heinkel from 4/KG 53 Haupt. H. Zollner
5 November	68	Mosquito TA 389	F. Sgt L. W. Neal F. Sgt E. Eastwood	
9 November	25	Mosquito	F. Lt J. Lomas F. Lt N.B. Fleet	Heinkel from 3/KG 53. Pilot O/Fhr W. Jansen
9 November	25	Mosquito MT 492	F.Lt D.H. Greaves F.O F.M. Robbins	Heinkel from 4/KG 53
9 November	125	Mosquito HK 263	F. Lt G.F. Simcock F.O N.E. Heijne	Heinkel from Gruppen Stab I Gruppe
11 November	68	Mosquito HK 348	F. Sgt A.R. P.O. R.B. Finn	Heinkel from 4/KG 53
19 November	456	Mosquito HK 246	F.O D.W. Arnold F.O J.B. Stickley	Heinkel from 5/KG 53 Pilot F/w R. Ripper
19 November	456	Mosquito HK 290	F.O. F.S. Stevens F.O W.A. Kellett	Heinkel from 1/KG 53 at 05.10 west of Texel
23 December	125	Mosquito HK 247	F. Lt R. W. Leggett F.O E.J, Midlane	Heinkel from 7/KG 53 Pilot Uffz. Robert Rosch
24 December	68	Mosquito TA 389	F. Sgt A. Bulles Obs T.W. Edwards	Heinkel from 7 KG 53 Pilot Lt H. Neuber

Total shot down by defensive squadrons above: 17

On 5 January 1945 a Heinkel from 9 KG 53 piloted by Hauptman S. Jessen was shot down by an unidentified intruder and another from Stab KG 53 was destroyed on the ground, also by an unidentified intruder.

Air-launched Flying Bombs Shot Down by Mosquito Fighters Over the North Sea

Date (1944)	Squadron	Crew	Notes
23/24 September	25	F.O. H.S. Cook F.Lt J. S. Limbert	Crew failed to return.
6/7 October	68	F. Lt H, Humphreys F.O. P. Robertson	Missile downed by use of fighter slipstream to upset robot control.
7/8 October	68	F. Lt H. Humphreys F.O. P. Burton	Downed two missiles, second by slipstream.
14/15 October	68	F.O. J.H. Haskell P.O. J. Bentley	Shot down two missiles.
19/20 October	68	W.O. D. Lauchlan F. Lt F. Bailey	Shot down two missiles.
19/20 October	68	F. Sgt A. Bulles F.O. L.W. Edwardes	

Date	Squadron	Crew	Notes
19/20 October	68	F.O. G.T. Gibson Sgt B.M. Lack	
19/20 October	125	F. Lt R.W. Leggett F.O. E.J. Midlane	
24/25 October	68	S. Ldr J.D. Wright F.O. J. McCulloch	Shot down two missiles.
25/26 October	68	S. Ldr M.J. Mansfield F. Lt S.A. Janacek	
25/26 October	68	Unidentified	
8/9 November	68	F.O. J.E. Ledwidge W/O C.A. Bonner	Shot down two missiles.
9/10 November	25	P.O. D.J. Carter P.O. W.J. Hutchings	Shot down two missiles.
10/11 November	25	P.O. D.J. Carter P.O. W.J. Hutchings	

After the middle of November instructions were given to Mosquito squadrons to ignore flying bombs and to concentrate on shooting down the Heinkel carriers.

APPENDIX XII

Air-launched Flying Bombs Shot Down by Tempest Fighters of 501 Squadron

Date 1944	Fuselage Code	Pilot	Location
4/5 September	SD-S	F/O K.V.Panter	Aldham, Essex
4/5 September	SD-Z	F/O R.C. Deleuze	Dedham, Essex
15/16 September	SD-M	F/O B.F. Miller	Two missiles shot down: Felsted and Latchingdon, Essex
24/25 September	SD-R	F/O B.F. Miller	Chigwell, Essex
28/29 September		F.Lt R.J. Lilwall	Barnston, Essex
5/6 October	SD-K	F/O J.A. Johnson	Romford, Essex
6/7 October	SD-Q	F/O R.C. Deleuze	Air-Burst
7/8 October	SD-L	F.Lt E.L. Williams	Two missiles shot down;Greenstead, Essex and Sutton, Kent
11/12 October	SD-L	F.Lt E.L. Williams	Felsted, Essex
12/13 October	SD-H	F.Lt G.R. Birbeck	River Blackwater
12/13 October	SD-J	F.Lt R. Bradwell	Great Coggeshall, Essex
13/14 October	SD-X	W/O E. Wojczynski	Great Bursted, Essex
14/15 October	SD-J	F/O. R.C. Deleuze	Two missiles shot down: Steeple and Nayland, Suffolk

Date	Fuselage Code	Pilot	Location
16/17 October		F/O R.H. Bennett	Ongar, Essex
17/18 October	SD-X	W/O E. Wojczynski	Thurrock, Essex
19/20 October	SD-J	F.Lt R. Bradwell	Hatfield, Herts.
19/20 October	SD-W	F/O. K.V. Panter	Two missiles shot down, Great Bentley and Fyfield, Essex
21/22 October	SD-Q	F/O R.C. Deleuze	Navestock, Essex
21/22 October	SD-R	F/O J.A.C. Johnson	Two missiles shot down; Rivenhall and Rayleigh, Essex
23/24 October	SD-P	F/O R.H. Bennett	Grays, Essex
23/24 October	SD-J	F/O D.A. Porter	Hartlip, Kent
24/25 October		F.Lt C.R. Birbeck	Latchingdon, Essex
25/26 October	SD-Y	F.Lt R.L.T. Robb	Downe, Kent
25/26 October	SD-U	F/O R.C. Stockburn	Margaretting, Essex
28/29 October	SD-L	F/O E.L. Williams	Danbury, Essex
30/31 October	SD-Y	F/O A.J. Grottick	Great Wigborough, Essex
4/5 Novemer	SD-L	F.Lt E.L. Williams	Ongar, Essex
4/5 November	SD-J	F.Lt D.A. Porter	Radwinter, Essex
8/9 November	SD-J	F.Lt R. Bradwell	Leadon Roding, Essex
8/9 November	SD-K	F.Lt D.A. Porter	South Stifford, Essex
9/10 November	SD-J	F.Lt R. Bradwell	Brentwood, Essex
10/11 November	SD-Z	F.Lt H. Burton	Writtle, Essex
10/11 November	SD-Z	F.Lt H. Burton	Great Warley, Essex
10/11 November	SD-V	F/O J. Maday	Hunsdon, Herts
22/23 November	SD-Z	F.Lt H. Burton	Harlow, Essex
23/24 November	SD-Z	F.Lt H. Burton	Springfield, Essex
5/6 December	SD-N	F.Lt H. Burton	Manuden, Essex
5/6 December	SD-P	S.Ldr A. Parker-Rees	Chignall, Essex
7/8 December	SD-K	F.Lt D.A. Porter	East Hornon, Essex
17/18 December	SD-N	W/O W.O. Balam	Newport, Essex
17/18 December	SD-Q	F/O R.C. Deleuze	Great Braxted, Essex
17/18 December	SD-G	W/O E. Wojcznski	Stebbing, Essex
17/18 December	SD-P	F.Lt R.J. Lilwall	Little Waltham, Essex
13/14 January 1945	SD-K	S.Ldr A.T. Langdon-Downs	North Cray, Kent

Between September 1944 and January 1945 forty-nine flying bombs were brought down by 501 Squadron.

501 Squadron Losses

Date 1944	Fuselage Code	Pilot	Location
23/24 September	SD-M	F/O G. Wild	Crashed near Colchester due to engine failure. Pilot baled out.
25/26 September	SD-L	F.Lt. G.L. Bonham	Flew into the ground. Pilot killed.
29/30 September	SD-E	F.Lt O.P. Farraday	Crashed at St Osyth, West of Clacton, due to engine failure. Pilot killed.
14/15 November	SD-S	F/O J.A. Johnson	Crashed at Standon, East of Bishop's Stortford, Herts., due to engine failure. Pilot baled out.

KG 3 and KG 53 Aircraft Losses During Air-launched Flying-bomb Operations

III/KG 3 operations between late June and 14 October 1944.

Sorties flown: approx. 700
Losses due to night-fighter action   5
Destruction on the ground by enemy action:
    at Beauvais/Tille   8
    at Handorf   4   12
Losses to other causes   <u>15</u>
                 Total 32

KG 53 operations between 15 October 1944 and 14 January 1945.

Sorties flown: approx. 750.

HQ Stab		I *Gruppe*	II *Gruppe*	III *Gruppe*	
HQ Stab/KH 53	1	1 *Staffel* 4	4 *Staffel* 7	7 *Staffel* 6	
HQ Stab/I *Gruppe*	1	2 *Staffel* 2	5 *Staffel* 3	8 *Staffel* –	
		3 *Staffel* 2	6 *Staffel* 3	9 *Staffel* 3	
	2	8	13	9	32
Loss by unidentified *Gruppe*					1
Total KG 53 losses					33

Total losses on air-launched operations from all causes were therefore sixty-five. One hundred Heinkel III H aircraft remained on the strength of KG 53 at the cessation of operations on 15 January 1945.

A statement by an interrogated POW that a further twelve Heinkel carriers were destroyed by the premature detonation of their V1 payloads is unsubstantiated and not taken into account in the above.

Accuracy of Air-launched Flying Bombs

The following statistics were provided by Air Ministry Scientists.

Target	Period	% Within 30 miles of target	Average deviation in line (miles)	Average deviation in range (miles)
London	18/19 July– 15/16 August	87	5.9	7.0
London	15/16 September– 29/30 September	44	8.5	5.4
London	5/6 October– 22/23 October	59	7.1	8.5
Manchester	24 December	63	9.9	9.0

Leaflets carried by Air-launched Flying Bombs

Date 1944/45	Location	Title of leaflet
4 November	Southminster, Marshes, Maldon, Essex	Not recorded
5 November	Frant, Sussex	The Other Side No. 1
9 November	East Grinstead, Sussex	The Other Side No. 1
15 November	Croydon	The Other Side
19 November	Carlton Colville, Suffolk	The Aftermath No. 6
19 November	Brickendon, Herts.	The Other Side
24 November	Dovercourt, Harwich	Not Recorded
25 November	Tendring, Great Bentley, Essex	A Splendid Decision
18 December	Radlett, Herts.	The Other Side No. 2
23 December	Oldbury, Ightham, Kent	*Signal* booklet and V1 PoW Post
23 December	Wokingham, Berks.	*Signal* and V1 POW Post
24 December	(Manchester raid) Turton; Oswaldtwistle; Oldham; Tottingham; Kelsal; Grange Moor; Rossington; Willerby	V1 POW Post No. 3
	Didsbury; Ollerton; Brindle	V1 POW Post No. 4
	Didsbury; South Cliffe	V1 POW Post No. 5
	Radcliffe; Worsley; Adswood	V1 POW Post No. 6
	Sturton le Steeple; Newport;	*Signal* Booklets
	Kelsal; Macclesfield Forest; Rossington; Epworth; Woodford	*Signal* booklet
14 January	Gravesend, Kent	The Other Side

Attachment of the FZG 76 Flying Bomb to the Heinkel Carrier Aircraft

1. The T shaped lifting lug on the flying bomb was the attachment point to the carrier aircraft.
2. The suspension point on the Heinkel carrier was located about 2.8 ft behind the rear spar. The weight of the bomb was probably spread between the front spar and the rear spar by a connecting structure.
3. The streamlined fairing covering the structure was unlike any other pylon used for the transport of large bombs by the Heinkel III. Except for the rear portion the fairing was wide and shallow, being only some 4 in deep at one point, but 1.7 ft wide at the widest point.
4. During flight the bomb was steadied by two telescopic rods which projected from the under-wing surface of the Heinkel and, under the starboard wing, was fixed 5 ft forward of the trailing edge. The rods terminated in a flat disk, approximately 7 in in diameter, which rested against the upper wing surface of the flying bomb.

    Two short arms were located near the front of the pylon and were separated at the fixture points by 2.4 ft. The arms were inclined forwards and inwards clasping the upper portion of the bomb just forward of the warhead.

5. An electrical connection, between the *zahl* apparatus and the spark plug on the Argus motor, was made by a cable that left the starboard side of the carrier aircraft via a 1 ft long metal tube. The cable had one right-handed coil and connected with the top of the spark plug under the cover of a conical cup, which served to protect the connection from the elements.

6. To initiate the starting procedure, compressed air was introduced into the system of the bomb by means of a connector between the Heinkel and the missile. Compressed air was probably discharged from a bottle located in or near the ventral cupola. A metal tube of streamlined cross-section and 0.8 in thick from front to rear projected horizontally for 8 in from the forward part of the cupola, then curved downwards at a right angle for a further 20 in. A strong hose carried the connection from here to the attachment point on the bomb. The whole link had a swivel attachment where it joined the carrier aircraft.

7. The area under the aircraft, where the bomb doors were located on other sub-types, was sheeted over with metal plating. These plates did not fit flush with the surrounding surfaces, but projected slightly on the front and sides. If the internal bomb containers were originally fitted, then these were removed to save weight.

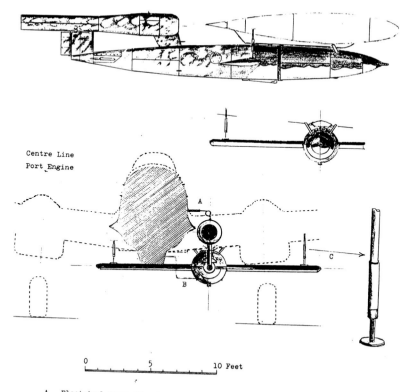

Centre Line
Port Engine

0   5   10 Feet

A   Electrical connection to sparking plug
B   Compressed air connection
C   Telescopic steadying strut   (Frank Leyland)

ATI 2nd TAF Aircraft Report No. 658, 27 April 1945 Heinkel III found on Kohlenbissen Airfield

This aircraft had been blown up and partly burned out but the equipment had remained surprisingly undamaged. Under the wing was a rack apparently designed to carry the flying bomb, with steadiers to bear against the wing and fuselage. Wireless carried consisted of FuG10p, Pe g 6, FuG BI, FuG 16z, FuG 25a, FuG 101a and FuG 217. The latter installation was retrieved and consisted of Mounting Frame, Receiver, Transmitter, Junction Box and Viewer. The aerials were placed on the trailing edge of the wing in front of the airleron, 2 m outboard of the flaps.

In the leading edge of the starboard wing was a rod about 4 ft 6 in long carrying at its forward end a small 2 bladed air log of coarse pitch, very similar to that on the flying bomb, but with shorter blades. Its use could not be ascertained.

The aircraft also carried a panel with equipment similar in appearance to that on the Ju 88 night fighter at Fassberg described in the airfield report No. 103/RAF. The main unit, however, bore the number Ln 132. The whole of this equipment has been salved and is being sent to England for examination.

Notes regarding the radio equipment are added here for explanation:

Pe g 6 – Peilgerat 6. Radio Compass

FuG 101a – Radio Altimeter

FuG B1 – Blind landing approach Receiver

FuG 10p – A variant which combined FuG 10 with the Peilgerat 6, a direction-finding set

FuG 16z – Radio communications equipment, the 16z being an amplified version of the basic set

FuG 25a – An Identification Friend or Foe (IFF) set developed and manufactured by GEMA. This set was used in conjunction with the Freya family of radars, the navigational aid system known by the code name 'Egon'

FuG 217 – A tail warning radar set for multi-engined aircraft. This had a maximum range of $2\frac{1}{2}$ miles.

Heinkel Carrier Crash Sites on Dutch Territory

① 8/KG 3. Heinkel 111 H-16. August 30/31.
② III/KG 3. Two Heinkel 111's collided. 04.30 hours, 18/19 September.
③ III/KG 3. Crashed near Vrouwenzand. 8/9 October.
④ 1II/KG 3. Two Heinkel 111's collided near Nijerirdum.
⑤ 5/KG 53. Heinkel 111 H-16. W.Nr. 162377, A1-NN. Crashed in Ijselmeer.
⑥ 1/KG 53. Heinkel 111 H-16. W.Nr. 160304, A1-BH. Crashed west of Texel.
⑦ KG 53. Heinkel 111 crashed at Callantsoog. Dead crew member washed up at a.

Bibliography

Documents

AIR 16/459: Operational Instructions about daylight attacks

AIR 16/610: Record of air-launched flying bomb operations 15 September 1944 to 16 January 1945

AIR 20/1661: Enemy methods of navigation for air launch. Report of AID (Science) dated 11 December 1944

AIR 20/2645: Expected scale of air-launched VI attack: War Cabinet 25 September 1944

AIR 20/3428: Report on incendiary-carrying flying bombs

AIR 20/3438: Airborne launches from the Low Coutries'. DD (Science) 7 August 1944

AIR 20/3685: Summary of flying bomb activity against the UK from 15 September 1944 to 29 March 1945

AIR 20/5348: Air defence of the UK: Proposals of 6 September 1944

AIR 27/293: Operational Record Book, 125 Squadron

AIR 27/307: Operational Record Book, 25 Squadron

AIR 27/604: Operational Record Book, 68 Squadron

AIR 27/604: Fighter Interception Development Squadron Report on the destruction of an air-launch Heinkel on 4 November 1944

AIR 27/1900: Operational Record Book, 456 Squadron

AIR 40/151: Royal Navy Port Liaison Officer's report on accounts given by trawler skippers who witnessed air launchings in the early hours of 24 December 1944

AIR 40/158: Reports from Allied agents about air launching; Report on Heinkel H-III captured at Kohlenbissen; Air launching trials at Peenemunde, POW Interrogation; Surviving crew of air-launch Heinkel taken 6 October, POW Interrogation; Possible modifications to Heinkel for air launch, reconnaissance photo interpretation

AIR 40/1653: List of VI incidents, on a daily basis, giving approximate positions

AIR 50/15: Combat Reports, Record Book 25 Squadron

AIR 50/48: Combat Reports, Record Book, 125 Squadron

Air Staff memorandum by HQ Fighter Command, 20 October 1944. Measures being taken to defeat the air launched offensive

Anti-Aircraft Command Paper 40511/13/G/WR of 21 October, 1944. Extension of diver strip to protect Midlands and West Riding from flying bomb attack

Friesche Luchvaart Documentatie, Leeuwarden, Netherlands; KG 3 and KG 53 losses

HO 193/35: Maps plotting fall of flying bombs on land and over the sea. Details of defensive action, times of incidents and wind strength and direction are included in some cases

HO 193/53: Map showing locations of air-launched flying bombs falling during the second phase. Not included in the plots are those shot down over the sea by Mosquito night fighters, two by AA and seven of the ten claimed by naval AA. Another three are not plotted because the positions were only roughly determined. A total of 608 bombs are plotted on the map and this figure is usually quoted for the number of non-abortive bombs

HO 198/93-96: Civil Defence Incident Reports for Regions 4, 5, 6 and 10. Region 5 is complete and includes small sketch maps for every incident. Region 4 is complete only for Essex and Suffolk. Reports for Region 6, except for a couple of incidents, are missing. Region 10 is complete for all VI incidents

HO 198/168: Form M2. List of VI incidents from 1 September to 31 October 1944. Date, time and map references are given and bombs shot down over the sea are included

HO 199/292: Leaflets discharged by flying bombs

HO 199/367: 'Unexploded flying bombs'

Notes on air launched diver activity in 12 Group area 18 September to 1 November 1944

War Cabinet subcommitee report to Chiefs of Staff dated 1 October, 1944: Deployment of AA guns in the box and eastern diver strip.

Books

Bowyer, Michael J.F. *Air Raid.* Patrick Stephens, 1979
Collier, Basil. *Air Defence of the United Kingdom.* HMSO, 1957
Comber, E.C. *Memoirs of a Spotter.*
Cooksley, Peter G. *Flying Bomb.* Charles Scribner, 1979
Erdmann, James D. *Leaflet Operations in the Second World War.*
Finn, S. *Lincolnshire Air War 1939 – 1945* Brayford Press
Hill, ACM Sir Roderic. *Report to the Secretary of State for Air.* Published as a supplement to the *London Gazette,* 19 October 1948
Howard-Williams, Jeremy. *Night Intruder.* David and Charles, 1976
Longmate, Norman *The Doodlebugs.* Hutchinson, 1981
O'Brien, T.H. *Civil Defence.* HMSO 1955
Pile, General Sir Frederick. *Ack-Ack.* George Harrap & Co, 1949
Rawnsley, C.F. and R. Wright. *Night Fighter* Collins, 1957
Wood, Derek. *Attack Warning Red.* London 1976
Young, Richard A. *The Flying Bomb.* Ian Allen, 1978

Index